ADDICTED

FEATURING **NEW ESSAYS** AND A **REVISED INTRODUCTION**

ADDICTED

NOTES FROM THE BELLY OF THE BEAST

edited by LORNA CROZIER *and* PATRICK LANE

GREYSTONE BOOKS

VANCOUVER/BERKELEY

To our companions in recovery

19 20 21 22 23 6 5 4 3 2

Greystone Books Ltd.
greystonebooks.com

Cataloguing data available from Library and Archives Canada

ISBN 978-1-77164-186-9 (PBK.)
ISBN 978-1-77164-187-6 (EPUB)

Editing by Barbara Pulling (first edition and third edition)
and Jan Walter (second edition)
Cover design by Peter Cocking
Text design and typesetting by Julie Cochrane,
Naomi MacDougall and Nayeli Jimenez
Printed and bound in Canada by Friesens
Distributed in the U.S. by Publishers Group West

Canadä

We gratefully acknowledge the financial support of the Canada Council for the Arts, the British Columbia Arts Council, the Province of British Columbia through the Book Publishing Tax Credit, and the Government of Canada through the Canada Book Fund for our publishing activities.

Greystone Books is committed to reducing the consumption of old-growth forests in the books it publishes. This book is one step towards that goal.

CONTENTS

INTRODUCTION

Over the past twenty-five years, I've sat in many a smoky kitchen with friends, all of us telling stories of parties, conferences, festivals and other events where we'd gathered as writers. There was always a bottle of wine in the middle of the table, a case of beer in the fridge, and a twentysix of whisky on the counter next to the sink. Funny and outrageous, our stories circled around booze and drugs, though the words *alcoholism* and *addiction* were never mentioned.

I don't regret the experiences we shared, but things are different now. The bottles may still be on kitchen tables and counters somewhere, but where I've been sitting for some time now, the spectre of addiction has added a cautionary note to our behaviour and our tales.

Some of Canada's most revered and influential writers—Margaret Laurence, Alden Nowlan, Gwendolyn MacEwen,

John Thompson, Marian Engel, Al Purdy, to name a few—were close companions of the bottle. In the United States, names like William Faulkner, Jack Kerouac, Raymond Carver and Dorothy Parker immediately come to mind. Sometimes you catch glimpses of this affinity in their fiction or poetry, but none of them left us with an autobiographical account. As I pondered the role alcohol has played in my own life, I couldn't help but wonder what these glorious writers would have said about the topic and what a difference their words might have made to those who read them.

Out of such ruminations came the idea for this book. The first name of my own generation that came to mind was David Adams Richards. David is not only a gifted writer but also a great raconteur. Some of the stories I've heard him tell in his rich New Brunswick lilt have been about his drinking days. Full of humour, self-deprecation and an incredible, charming honesty, they hold listeners enthralled. If he agreed to put his words on paper, I thought, I'd take it as a sign to approach others. I hesitated to phone him. Talking around the table and writing things down for the whole world to see are very different propositions. But David's response to my request was an immediate "Great idea." He said that though he'd written about alcoholism in his novels, he'd never done so in a more personal account, and it was "about time" he did.

David's "about time" confirmed my sense that this was the right moment for such a book. After he accepted, I asked my companion, Patrick Lane, to share the task of editing and to write an essay. For twenty years, we'd been living with his struggles to get sober. Our mutual breaking of the silence around alcoholism became an act of faith. If we were going to ask others to find words for their demons, we needed to do it ourselves.

There are more than two hundred types of twelve-step groups in North America. Though the addictions they address vary from alcohol to food to emotional crises, all emphasize the necessity of anonymity. When you walk into that church basement or community centre, you are guaranteed that what you say and who you are will remain behind closed doors. The writers who accepted our invitation to compose an original piece for *Addicted* broke this first rule. They stepped out, gave their full names, and put their lives on the line. I can't emphasize enough the courage of this act.

—

THOSE WHO KNOW little about substance abuse see it as something unsavoury and shameful. Why don't the drunks, the junkies, the smokers, the bulimics just smarten up? Pull themselves up by the bootstraps. Get some willpower. Stop. There's also a touch of the romantic about the wild, self-destructive painter or poet who shatters conventions and taboos. Counteracting these simplistic attitudes toward addiction, the contributors to this collection give us the bare bones of their reality. Several said that writing about this part of their lives gave them new insights into where they had been and what they had become. That was an advantage none of us had predicted. Most had agreed to take the risk in the hope that their stories would help someone else. That, indeed, has happened. In the years since the first publication of *Addicted: Notes from the Belly of the Beast* in 2001, we've become aware of a growing number of readers who have been helped by the honesty and poignancy of these stories.

We've received hundreds of emails and letters from people in recovery and from family members who walk a parallel path in that journey. Often the book was a gift, an antidote to despair, from mothers and fathers, from sisters and husbands. It was passed from hand to hand at treatment centres. A university criminologist told us he uses *Addicted* in his classes to bring to light the personal side of addiction, one that gets lost in statistics and academic texts. A nurse who approached us on a ferry said she bought copies for several young people she knows, including her son, who are struggling with a combination of drug abuse and mental illness. We heard the story of a Toronto visual artist who, to escape the censure of his girlfriend, packed himself and four bottles of vodka off to a lakeside cabin for the weekend. At the kitchen table, glass in hand, he turned the radio on and listened to an interview by Shelagh Rogers on the CBC. Peter Gzowski was the guest this time rather than the host, along with Patrick, Marnie Woodrow and me. We were talking about the book. At the end of the interview, the artist phoned his girlfriend, told her where he was and what he was doing and asked her to pick him up. He wrote Patrick in care of the publisher to tell him that Patrick's story had changed his life. One day at a time he was getting sober.

That kind of response and the selling out of the initial printing made us publish a second edition of *Addicted: Notes from the Belly of the Beast* with three additional essays in 2006. And now we're doing it again. At the demand of readers and with the support of the publisher, we're not only keeping the book alive but enriching it once again by including three essays. LesLIE, Elianna Lev and Tom Bissell have added bracing new material that affirms the importance of candid, front-of-the-line writing about the dangers and afflictions that can crush a life. This expanded version marks the fifteenth anniversary of the first edition. We think that's something to celebrate.

The books that readers cherish make them feel less alone. No one is lonelier than addicts and those who love them. The majority of the writers here share an addiction to alcohol; in our culture that remains the common drug of choice.

It is, after all, legal and easy to get. The other contributors write about smoking, cocaine, heroin, marijuana, gambling, gaming, sexual addiction and an obsession with food and pharmaceuticals. But whatever their demons, these writers offer a view of a world rarely seen in our literature. Because they were brave enough to speak openly about their experiences, without self-pity or false justifications, their words break through the isolation and loneliness that addiction creates. Sometimes what they have to say is harrowing, disturbing, but each story is a gift, offering the possibility of healing and hope.

LORNA CROZIER

ADDICTED

COUNTING THE BONES

PATRICK LANE

I START ON MY KNEES. It's the position of prayer, but an alcoholic neither knows nor understands prayer. I am naked and my knees press into the clean white tiles. My forearms rest on the rim of a mottled white bowl. It is six o'clock in the morning in a hotel somewhere in Toronto. I don't remember the name of the hotel. It's just a hotel, a place of anonymous safety, a continent away from where I live. My hands grip the toilet bowl as I dry-heave yet again, there being nothing in my stomach to throw up except for a few glaucous strings of phlegm. They hang from my lips until they fall into the bowl in turgid knots. I stare into a sea where nothing lives. My abdomen tightens into a fist and punches at my stomach as it tries to force out what is no longer there, the alcohol of the long, pitiful night.

I heave again and again, unable to stop this belly cramp. I'm crying, but I'm not aware of that, not yet. Tears and sweat are much the same after you've drunk thirty ounces of alcohol and snorted two grams of cocaine. Three more surges and the first blood comes, a few drops that splash into the snot-skewed water. They drop and flower there like the lost blossoms of a geranium, a heavy red, bright with oxygen. They are like the blossoms that grow on the fists of a man who strikes a cement wall so he can feel something, anything, himself. It is blood from an artery. I see this and wonder at it as I heave again. There is in my mind a kind of grim amusement at this flowering. I would laugh if I could. The next spasm brings more, a tablespoon of blood that drowns the delicate flowers that shimmered there a moment before. I am somehow sorry to see them go. Another, and my mouth fills with blood. It boils across my tongue, through my lips and into the bowl.

My body shakes and trembles with a terrible palsy. I am covered with thin sweat. My feet and hands are cold. It is as if my heart can't find the way to fuel those parts of me that shine out into touching. There is no feeling in them. They hang from my limbs like the heavy books my teachers used to make me hold at arm's length to punish me. When my arms could no longer hold the books out straight, I was strapped for weakness.

When was that?

Too long ago.

I get up carefully, wipe my face with a stained washcloth, and stumble to the bed. I sit down heavily, stare past my belly at my flaccid sex, my thighs and feet. They belong to someone else. I balance precariously. I can't lie down. Not yet. I take a cigarette from the packet on the bedside table, light it, and pull blue smoke into my lungs. I feel the dizziness as my arteries contract, and I almost faint. I am rocking slowly but I'm unaware of that, just as I'm unaware of my tears. It is a rocking in time with my beating heart.

I look back at the bedside table and reach for the bottle of vodka. I unscrew the white plastic cap, lift the bottle to my lips, and take a small drink, anything to stop the shakes and nausea. I have already forgotten about the blood. It's as if the vomiting occurred somewhere in the deep past, so long ago it is barely remembered by the animal I am. The alcohol slides past my acid-burned throat and hits my stomach like a rock striking thin water. The liquor sits there for a brief moment and then I'm back on my knees by the toilet bowl, puking again. There is only a little blood this time. I feel relieved and yet somehow disappointed. Surely there is more blood in me than that? What's wrong with my body that it will not obey?

Back to the bed, where I lift the cigarette from the ashtray, almost burned down to the filter, take a drag, and then pick up the bottle again, swallowing two or three ounces. I know I have to get the alcohol past my stomach and into my intestines, where it can be absorbed by my bloodstream. Only then will I feel better. It works. This time my stomach holds on, and in a minute or two I feel the drowsy steadiness in my muscles and brain. My body slows and the nausea begins to disappear. I take another drink and then another, until I have six or seven ounces in me. Only then do I lie down, light another cigarette from the last one, and stare over my feet at the city as it begins its terrible anonymous day. The traffic noise is a vague and persistent buzz.

There is no more cocaine. I check the wrappers, but they have been licked clean sometime in the night. My nose is bleeding now, the small sores cracked open by my puking. In four hours I have an interview on national radio and in six hours with a national newspaper. I have a reading at eight o'clock tonight in a bar somewhere off Yonge Street. I close my eyes, not to sleep, but to lie in the dark of my body.

The heavy drinking has begun again, but it's never really stopped. I've been dry-drunk a few weeks here and there in the past three years. Dry-drunk. An alcoholic waiting until he can drink again. I think of the word *wrath*, the word *punishment*, the word . . . what word? Why not joy, contentment, serenity, peace?

—

TWO MONTHS LATER, I sit in my office and try to remember when my addiction started. That's what it is: an addiction, a disease. I try to remember my first drink, but it's too far away, lost in clouds and rain. Perhaps it was in my mother's womb, or passed to me in my mother's milk. It could have been the sips of beer my mother or father gave me as a child when they were drinking. I loved the taste of beer, the froth, the bubbles, so different from orange pop or Coca-Cola. I know I was thirteen when I had my first serious drink. My parents had left me home to baby-sit on New Year's Eve. While my sister and brother slept, I opened the liquor cupboard beside the fridge. Inside were vodka, rye whisky, dark Navy rum and lemon gin.

I got a tumbler from beside the sink and poured some of each bottle into the glass until it was full. I drank the liquor quickly out of fear I would be caught. I was instantly, totally drunk, and I loved the feeling. Within ten minutes I was in the back yard, throwing up in the garden. When I finished puking I went back into the kitchen, poured another glass full of the mix of liquors, and drank it. This time I didn't vomit. How much did I keep down? Probably five or six ounces. Thinking of it now, I wonder I didn't kill myself. Instead, I simply stumbled upstairs to bed and passed out.

Did I inherit this madness? Was it in my father's seed or my mother's egg? What history I know of my family on both sides is terrible, full of the dead and the dying, the raging, the infirm, a man, my grandfather, drunk, burying my father's mother, my grandmother, under a caragana hedge so she would be of use and fertilize the earth on the farm near Pincher Creek, Alberta. Why let her body go to waste in a graveyard? Or so my grandfather thought. My father ran away from home shortly afterwards. He was thirteen. There are too many stories, too much for me to remember. I sat drunk with my mother when she was drunker, two years after my father was murdered, her telling me of their life together, stories I should never have heard, her raising her skirt to her pudenda and saying, Daddy always called me Hairless

Joe. I didn't know if it was my father or her father she spoke of, mumbling from her chair, her white thighs glaring in the lamplight, her shaking hands gripping her whisky, my sorrow.

As a teenager I was full of pretension about literary things. I thought William Blake's line from his *Proverbs*, "The road of excess leads to the palace of wisdom," meant that, in order to achieve wisdom, you must live with complete abandon. Sex, drugs, the wild dance; a lack of tolerance, wisdom, grace. I had confused Blake with Rimbaud. But it didn't matter. Nothing did.

Strange how you remember things: Saturday night in the mid-fifties, with a case of beer bought from the Capitol Taxi bootlegger. I drank it all in a few hours with friends and then drove off alone in search of a girl, any girl, a dirt road, a car parked under slow lonesome trees and tearing off my clothes as she tore hers off and making, what? Love, perhaps, or what I thought love was back then, drunken, crazy sex without any responsibility for her or for myself. Elvis Presley had just reinvented the world. Rock 'n' roll, the postwar bounty years awash with money, my father with a new car, a house he owned, me striding through school with Ezra Pound and Eliot on my mind, arrogant and confused. I drank every weekend and sometimes during the week if I could get a half-case of beer or a mickey. Sometimes I shared the liquor, but most times I drank it alone.

The daily drinking began in my early twenties. I was married with three kids by then and there wasn't much money for liquor, but when there was the smallest amount left over it went for cheap wine or a bottle of port that I sipped at to make last as long as possible, a night or two at most, while I sat up late struggling with my wretched early poems. The sixties almost finished me. It was a decade of death and loss starting with my brother's little girl, five years old, dying of cancer. That was 1962. In 1964, my brother, older than I by three years, died in Vancouver of a brain hemorrhage. He was a poet as well, one of the wild Lane boys of myth and legend. My family reeled at the deaths. I think I went mad then, but so did we all, two other brothers, a sister, my mother. Four years later my father was gunned down at his office by a drunken customer with a grudge. My mother-in-law had died only a few weeks earlier.

Three months after my father's death I got up from the kitchen table and walked out the door, leaving my wife and children behind. I had eight dollars in my pocket and the shirt on my back. I have only fragments of memory from that time: a huge rainstorm east of Calgary and me lying in a ditch, drenched and shaking; the dusty roads of Saskatchewan; the cars and trucks that picked me up and took me across the country. On the University of Toronto campus I bought a collection of Garcia Lorca's poems with my last, sad dollar. I read it on the lawn surrounded by students walking to their classes.

I stayed in Toronto through the spring and summer, living on the street, drinking what I begged or stole in the bars on Spadina and Queen, until I hitchhiked west and reappeared at my front door in Vancouver. My marriage lasted four more months. We split up, my wife remarried, and I was gone. I had a beater of a car, a thousand dollars I'd borrowed from my mother, a fifty-pound Remington typewriter in the trunk with a sheaf of canary-yellow paper, and a couple of bottles of whisky on the seat beside me. I was headed directly for self-destruction.

The next few years I wandered the continent in a blur of casual affairs, casual friendships, communards and hippies, criminals and crazies. I lived in a series of crippled Volkswagen vans in various stages of repair, or in the apartment of whichever girl was willing to put up with me for a week or two while I ate her food and enjoyed her body. I slept in alleys, in cardboard boxes, on rooftops, surviving through the usual petty crimes and misdemeanours. I belonged nowhere. I was utterly alone and I wanted it that way: just me, a bottle, a bag of drugs. That I wrote book after book of poems during this time leaves me bewildered now. I was completely addicted to alcohol by then. The drugs I could take or leave: opium, hashish, grass, cocaine, acid, amphetamines. They were decorations on the Christmas tree bottle that was always with me.

—

WHERE DOES ALL this leave me now, in my sixty-first year? Still addicted, moving from abstinence to excess and back to abstinence at a rate that would stagger most people or kill them, ranging through shame, guilt, self-pity, anger, despair, doubt and confusion.

I have a disease. Ten years ago I would have laughed at such a notion. Booze and drugs and tobacco are available everywhere, and I choose to use them. But what do I do when they start using me? What do I do when I'm on my knees puking blood, only to go right back to the bottle? The straight and sane people of this ordinary world have little time for drunks and users. Addicts and alcoholics steal and lie and cheat. Sometimes they maim or kill. They can't be trusted by anyone, least of all themselves. Their souls are drowned in a bottle or rolled up in a five-dollar bill. They travel through remorse until it sticks like a bone in their throats. They ask for forgiveness only to betray it ten minutes later in a bar with a second double chilling in a shaky hand.

I've been there. I know that place.

A lot of my friends are addicts and alcoholics, people who live in excess, their bodies driven by what owns them. Given the moment, given the particular day or night, given the desperation, most of them would sell their mothers for a bottle, an eight-ball, a paper or two of heroin and a needle. Some are in jail or in rehab centres. Some are dead. The writers and artists of this country who've wasted their talents and their lives are legion. Gwendolyn MacEwen, Milton Acorn, but so many others. Johnny hanging from an electrical cord in the Blackstone Hotel on Granville Street; Jimmy dead with a needle still in his arm two weeks out of rehab, overestimating his tolerance, his body wrapped around a toilet in Chinatown; Debra selling herself to anyone for another trip to the shooting gallery, her eyes filled with pitiful, sordid despair, until she was found in a dumpster in Montreal.

I know where they've been because I've been there. The spectres, the ghosts live with me. I only have to go back and remember and the madness returns. I see myself driving down the frozen midnight highway somewhere in British Columbia with one eye closed, because the road ahead veers off wildly in two directions. I drive like that for three hundred miles, my eyelid practised at the manoeuvre, then suddenly find myself in a field fifty miles west of Prince George with barbed wire wrapped across my spidered windshield like coiled ribbons, my head bleeding from hitting the wheel.

Or is it two years later, my car rolling on the 401, the third accident in four months? In each accident I've lost consciousness. This time my car catches the gravel as I pass a semi. The tires crack to the side and the car heels over and up and I say to myself, This time I want to stay awake and see what it's like, full of drunken bravado. But after the third roll I'm unconscious again. I awake to a guy speaking quietly to me through the side window of the upside-down car: "Jesus, you okay? You rolled eight times." I'm angry. I saw only three rolls before I was out. Whisky and wine drip from the ceiling, there's glass everywhere. The Ontario police escort me to a little local hospital and then let me go, why, I'll never know.

My Quebec licence plates, maybe. The hospital kicks me out with a broken collarbone. Bits of glass glaze my cheeks and hands. Go back to your own province, they say. Get treated there. I stagger out into the night and through the streets of some lost little nowhere town, find the highway west, and start walking, the wind hard off Lake Ontario. In ten hours I'm in Toronto, drinking in a cheap hotel room with a girl who's struggling with my belt and zipper while I take just one more drink from her bottle. She's some hippie girl from England, stoned herself, the Summer of Love just a few short years behind both of us.

I sit here in the night and I count my shattered bones. It's as good a way as any to chart my life. Everything seems to begin with the broken. Two toes, but I was only a boy, so they don't count. A shattered ankle, the doctor happy, he tells me, because he only gets two or three breaks this bad in a lifetime. Your ankle's cornflakes, he says, and puts it together with fifteen pins. A stoned, drunken jump off a thirty-foot cliff into shallow water at my mother's seventy-fifth birthday reunion. Right leg broken, hit by a car outside a bar. A clean break, though, with friendly nurses. Four lumbar vertebrae, same cliff jump, except the doctors didn't notice the compression fractures then. Three cervical vertebrae, discovered ten years later by my chiropractor. I'm shorter now by an inch or two. Third finger, left hand, setting chokers up on Sugar Lake, hungover and tired. Both forearms, multiple fractures, not drunk, simply foolish as a boy in high school.

Collarbone from the Highway 401 crash, left shoulder distorted one inch. Shoulder blade, slipping as I stumbled drunk downstairs. Broken nose in a barroom fight, one punch by a kid not as drunk as me and then down on the floor looking for my glasses. Concussion from falling out a window onto my head. Scars? Too many to count. Injuries that should've killed me but didn't through some crazed good luck. God protects the drunk and the stupid.

But that's only my body. What else have I broken? Families, wives, children, lovers, friends, brothers, sister, mother, father. They wander out there. Or maybe they don't, and I am locked again in self-pity and ego, thinking I have changed the world by my actions, my endless preoccupation with myself. And is all this confession excessive? Am I healing here?

The past is a burden I carry on my shoulder. On the other shoulder is the future. Right here is this one moment, twisting perfectly as it must in the is-ness of now. And now what? Go back and find the dead, to murmur my loss in whispers of dust? Take into my arms my niece, my brother, my father and wish them alive again; gather my children, my grandchildren, my friends and tell them I am sorry? Kneel at my woman's feet and beg forgiveness? Sorrow is a root that grows from the heart, and the heart has no cure but love. I suffer, but who does not?

I am confused and sometimes dismayed at what the world is, now I am recovering. Ice and snow, vodka and cocaine. Stand on a street corner in any city and watch for a moment as drugs change hands, a hooker working her life away to pay for her pimp's habit and her own. Look for the men who stand in the shadows as they wait for the liquor store to open, hiding ten steps away from the sound of a door unlocking. After you've done that, go to a place where you can walk into a room, sit down, and, when it comes your turn, say, Hello, I'm Patrick. I'm an alcoholic. Start by telling your story to others, the ones who know where you have been, as you pray for the years before and behind you, the year you're living now, the night, the day, this hour, this minute, this one.

MY FATHER, MYSELF

MARNIE WOODROW

LOOKING BACK, I can see that I had several fathers. Some of them were easier to love than others. I've been different people at different times in my life, too. And some of them were easier to *be* than others. My father drank too much and, for a time, so did I. Something made him continue to drink; something made me pause halfway along the path.

There's a man in a black snowsuit and a red toque: I call him Daddy. His cheeks are chubby, pink from the cold. He tows me up and down a snow-covered hill, pulling the toboggan with big strong arms. He gives in to me whenever I beg, "One more time, plee-ease!" and then carries me all the way home on his shoulders. I spend Saturday afternoons watching him fix cars as he laughs with his friends. He has a lot of friends in our small town. I decide he's famous because he owns a garage.

I'm in charge of sweeping the floors of the garage with a big push broom. Left alone with a seemingly endless supply of pale-blue paper, I draw pictures in a room that smells of motor oil and axle grease. I write my name over and over and make up stories. I know the words *carburetor*, *alternator*, *starter* and *alignment*, although I can't yet write them down. If I'm good, my daddy takes me across the street to his friend's garage, where they have a rack that lifts cars right off the ground. I ride up and down on the rack, knowing my mother would be furious if she saw me doing this. Then one day my daddy's garage isn't a place we go to any more. My mother tells me it belongs to someone else now. Oh. When we drive past it I feel sad. I hate the people who took it away from my daddy. He seems to hate them too.

I'm a little older: he's Dad now. He teaches me to throw and catch a baseball; he teaches me to bait a hook without crying. Sometimes I think he forgets that I'm a girl; I go into the house wailing because he hits me with a puck while we're playing hockey on the rink he made for me in our yard. My voice is accusatory as I tell my mother, "Dad tried to kill me!" But I still know that this is the man who buys me chips and gum just because I ask. He watches baseball games on a black-and-white TV that he carries outside and plugs into the exterior wall of the house. While the announcer shouts out "Home Run!" and "Bases Loaded!", my dad fixes our car even if it isn't broken. He stays out there in the dark, by the light of the flickering television, a cooler of beer at his feet. He works for someone else now, selling car parts from behind a counter. He's not happy when he comes to the dinner table carrying a bottle of beer. I tell him at least now he can keep his fingernails clean, but he doesn't smile. The bottle of beer is always beside him, cold and salty. Sometimes he lets me have a sip.

Our house is situated at the bottom of a hill where two streets merge. My dad sits on a lawn chair on the front porch, sipping beer and frowning. Cars come racing down the hill and sometimes they don't quite stop at the stop sign. My dad runs into the street shouting "Hey!" and "Stop!!!", waving his fist. His anger lasts for hours. He keeps a pen handy to write down the licence plate numbers of the offending cars. I try not to be in the yard when he does these things. He's usually a soft-spoken man, but when he yells my stomach turns to ice water. I've never heard anyone sound so angry before. I pray that he will never yell at me like that. I decide he's angry because he doesn't have a job. He "lost" it. I now know that he lost the garage, too. A lot of things seem to be going missing these days. My mother promises me that everything is fine; she tells me that my dad is angry about the cars that don't quite stop because he's worried one of the kids in the neighbourhood will be killed by *one of those jerks*. Oh.

The man I call Dad smells like mouthwash, stale sweat and onions. His shirt isn't tucked in, his nose is red like Rudolph's. He tells me to wait in the car because he has to "pick something up." I wait and wait. It's getting dark outside and I'm bored. I stare at the bottle of Scope on the floor of the car. Apparently my dad is very worried about having bad breath. I read advertising flyers out loud in the dim light and hunt for candies and gum, singing to myself. For a man without a job he seems to have a lot of errands. When we pull out of the parking lot he drives so slowly I want to scream. I don't realize that he's worse than the people who don't stop at the stop sign in front of our house, that he's drunk as he drives me all over town. All I know is that he doesn't laugh or smile very much, and if I whine he gets mad and tells me I'm a baby.

When we get home my mother looks at him as if she doesn't like him any more. Sometimes I think she's being mean to him; other times I can see that she's been crying. "Where the hell were you?" she hisses in a cracked voice. When she kisses me and tucks me in, she asks me where I went with Dad. I usually say "We went to Peter's House." Peter's House is synonymous with driving home on the wrong side of the road. I hear the words *I can't take much more, Bill* echoing through the house late at night. I lie awake listening for the sound of my mother packing a suitcase and leaving me behind. She doesn't, but I never stop worrying about it.

My dad loves me. My mother tells me this over and over. He's having a hard time right now, that's all. She buys him a beautiful blue suit and a leather briefcase. He looks fat and handsome in his suit, but I don't know why he needs a briefcase. He doesn't seem to like working; if he gets a job, he loses it. I'm not supposed to think that my dad's bad moods have anything to do with me. I'm a good girl; he loves me and everything is going to be fine. But I'm worried we're going to have to move to the Poor House. My mother takes me with her whenever she goes to visit friends. Her friends don't come to our house because it's a pigsty. I learn the word *ashamed*, which is much easier to spell than carburetor. My dad isn't always very nice. He calls my friend Charles a *bloody pansy*. Charles hears him, and I never bring a friend home with me again.

When I go downstairs to watch cartoons my dad is there, asleep on the sofa. He's cranky if I wake him up, so I try not to. The only time he doesn't sleep on the downstairs sofa is when my grandpa comes to visit. Before Grandpa arrives my mom and I clean the house for hours. My dad is very messy, and my mother likes things to be tidy. I think this must be why they fight so much. I keep my room neat and try to stay in it for as long as possible. The rest of the house doesn't feel good. I draw and write a lot, because every other game seems too noisy against the silence. My parents get along better when my grandpa's around. I wish he would come and live with us so my mother would be happy like that every day. She loves her daddy. I wish I could love mine without trying.

We go to church on Sundays because God is going to help my father drink less beer. The basement fridge is full of big bottles of Pepsi and 7-Up. My dad has a bookmark that says"God grant me the serenity to accept the things I cannot change, the courage to change the things I can, and the wisdom to know the difference." I don't know what it means, but I like the sound of it. My dad has a psychiatrist. He goes to AA meetings and something called *therapy*. I go to meetings too. At them I meet kids whose fathers beat them up and threaten them with knives, whose mothers hide bottles of vodka in the broom closet. These kids talk about the terrible things they have seen. They laugh as they brag about all the times they've poured their father's booze down the drain. I think: I don't belong here. My dad doesn't hit us and we still have money for food. Dad says he has stopped drinking forever and I believe him. He wasn't an alcoholic; he just liked his beer.

One morning I wake up early and go outside. My father's car is parked in the middle of the flower bed on our front lawn, and he's asleep in the driver's seat. A few weeks later, when my mother and I are out in the car, we find a bottle of rum in his leather briefcase in the trunk; my mother pours it out on the side of the road, cursing. I come home early from school one afternoon to find my nondrinking father with a bottle of beer in his hand and an angry, caught look on his face. He shouts at me to go away and play with my friends. Whenever I get home from school after that, I hold my breath when I turn the doorknob.

My mother tells me she has been to see a lawyer. She arranges for me to wait at a baby-sitter's house on weekdays until she gets home from work, and one afternoon she comes late to pick me up. She says my father's had an accident. I think she means in the car and start crying. Once we're home she tells me to pack a bag so that I can stay over at the babysitter's house that night. I see strange stains on the white carpet in our living room, more stains on the stairs leading up to my room. Blood. I find out that my father fell down the stairs and cut his head after he opened my mother's mail from the lawyer. He wasn't drinking Pepsi that day.

My mother and I leave; we come back. Things are pleasant for a while, then ugly. I despise the man who lives in our basement; his hugs and kisses make me cringe. He's sweaty and slams doors, swears and makes my mother cry herself to sleep. This man is a liar who swerves and stumbles when he walks. He falls asleep drunk, leaving pans of food burning on the stove. I think, We're going to die here. He's not my real father, I say to my mother. I use her words: *I can't take much more of this.* I tell her that I don't want to stay there, that I'll run away if she doesn't get us out soon. She hears me loud and clear, and we move into a one-bedroom apartment. The new owners of our house call the police because my father won't leave peacefully.

Yet another sort of father appears in my life. This one lives in a motel on the side of a highway, in a room crammed with things from our old house. He's three hours late for every visit and drunk when he arrives. Now that I don't have to live with him, I feel sorry for him. I know what he really means when he says he has the flu. Pity has replaced love. Sometimes it even replaces the hate. I agree to see him, even though he scares me half to death by driving past our apartment building at odd hours, looking up at our windows. I get in the car with him and try not to breathe through my nose so that I won't smell the mouthwash, or the booze under it. I beg a God I don't believe in to keep the car from crashing while I'm in it. I remember my mother shouting at my father, *If you want to kill yourself, that's one thing.*

My mother and I move to the suburbs of a nearby city with her future husband. After I graduate from high school, my mother decides to move back to my hometown; I stay in the city and begin to build a life of my own. My father comes to visit me, and we both pretend he doesn't have a drinking problem, never did. He orders Diet Coke in restaurants. Shortly after my nineteenth birthday, we go out for supper. I order a beer, and my father is startled. I enjoy the look on his face, the fear and longing. I want him to admit that he wants a drink, too, or that he had seven drinks before he came to pick me up. We keep seeing each other, keep having conversations about nothing much. I feel a vague flicker of love for him when he cries at sad movies; I am slowly recognizing the traces of my father that are present in me. We're both "too sensitive." We both cough if we laugh too hard. We both love music.

My father and I look alike, with our dark thick eyebrows and wavy hair, the same boyish jaw. But he is gaunt, with the distended stomach of the chronic alcoholic. His skin is sallow, a mix of yellow and grey that makes me burst into tears as soon as he drives away. He puts off having an operation he needs because he doesn't trust doctors. He's been in and out of hospital a few times over the years for what he seems to think are mysterious ailments. There's no mystery about it: my father is drinking himself to death. The closest I come to addressing this fact is to say "Behave yourself, Dad" when I hug him good-bye. I tell him that I'll come look after him if he decides to have the operation, that I'll clean up his apartment while he's in the hospital. A part of me is enraged that I offer this, but I do. I feel responsible for my father in a way that sickens me. He often reminds me that I am the centre of his universe, brings me groceries, and tries to make up for all the times he's let me down. I am furious with him as he limps along beside me, but something in me can't say so. On the outside I am the smiling daughter. And I am starting to forgive him, slowly, if only because I still entertain the hope that we'll have a real talk about why he threw his life away, and part of mine with it. I can feel him getting ready to tell me something when he admits he "let everything slide" after my mother and I left him.

I can drink quite a lot of beer myself by now, and I see why he likes it so much. I drink with my friends as often as I can, on every kind of occasion. I've started writing, and that gives me plenty of reasons to drink, too. I have cocktails to recover from the nervous tension of public readings, drinks to celebrate the launch of someone else's book, more drinks to console myself after being turned down by yet another magazine. My heroes are Tennessee Williams (addict, dead), Dorothy Parker (addict, dead), Raymond Carver (recovered alcoholic who died of cancer resulting from chain-smoking). My public or "literary" drinking self is not as separate from my solitary drinking self as I like to imagine. I feel increasingly lonely, whether I am surrounded by people or hidden away in my apartment with a case of beer. Like my father before me, I begin to prefer the latter. Cooking, usually one of my main passions, is now done at 3 A.M, and *gourmet* is not a word I'd use to describe the results. Breakfast is a pot of coffee and a handful of Tylenol. But I feel sure, or maybe just determined, that I'll never end up like my father. I have a job, I pay my bills, and I am never late for anything, no matter what. I follow two unspoken rules: never drink when I'm feeling sad or angry, and *never* drink at the typewriter. Drinking is something I do for fun, not because I need to. My love of beer is only that: a love of beer.

I'm working sixty hours a week in a restaurant kitchen, and yet I finally feel like my life is coming together. My second book is due out soon and I live like a real writer—drinking, smoking, and hanging out with other artists. I'm twenty-five years old and a published author, full of hope and ideas and a beautiful arrogance.

It's a busy Friday night at the restaurant where I work. The kitchen is hectic, the dining room jammed to capacity. I look forward to the end of the night, because that's when the staff sits around drinking, winding down from the chaos. As a prep cook it's my job to make sure all the chefs have what they need: chopped veggies, olive oil, minced garlic, melon balls, whipped cream. I have to hustle to keep up. The phone rings, and someone shouts that the call is for me. I give the head chef an apologetic look and stomp off to answer it.

My girlfriend and I have just broken up, so I'm surprised to hear her voice on the line. She tells me I have to call the police in my hometown right away, or my aunt. "Which aunt?" I hear myself shouting, terrified that something has happened to my mom. I haven't told either of my parents that my love life has fallen apart (again), and they don't know where to reach me. I hang up and call the friend I'm staying with, ask her to look up my aunt's number in my phone book. "You need to call your mother right away," my friend says. "What the fuck is going on?" I yell into the phone. Everyone working in the kitchen looks at me. "Your dad died," she says softly. "Please call your mom." Someone is screaming, and I realize it's me.

The chef ushers me into the back office and brings me a drink. I gulp it down, bitterly aware of the irony of this remedy. My father drank himself to death: to comfort myself I am sucking down a triple Scotch. I ask for another. Oh, well, I'm upset, I think. Who wouldn't have a drink at a time like this? I tell myself the same thing as I stop to buy a six-pack of beer on my way home. The first of my unspoken rules about drinking, Never drink when feeling sad or angry, is easily ignored. I don't know it yet, but a new rule has taken its place: *always* drink if I'm feeling either thing.

My father is now a photograph sitting on a casket. He is clothing in a closet, dirty dishes in a sink, stacks of video cassettes and an abundant cache of frozen foods. Here but not here, just as he was throughout my childhood, only now he is absent in that most final of ways.

At the visitation and the funeral I hear countless stories about a man I had almost forgotten. It's as if the daddy who pulled the toboggan up and down the hill as many times as I asked, who laughed till tears ran down those chubby cheeks, is suddenly back in the room. He was such a nice guy, people say, a wonderful uncle. He was so passionate about helping kids. Was, used to be. What I hear breaks my heart. Something beautiful in my father had been destroyed long before his life actually ended. He was fifty-six, and it had taken him years to get what he seemed to have been looking for: the freedom to kill himself with nobody watching.

When the time comes to sort through his belongings, I refuse help from his sisters. I feel pretty certain he wouldn't like a whole bunch of people touching his stuff. I also hope—in vain—that some sort of message will present itself as I go through his trove of photographs, mementos and papers. It's a daunting task. My father wasn't just messy, he was compulsively so. He lived his last years in squalor. Upgrading from roadside motels to an apartment building in town hadn't altered his indifference to housekeeping. I work in a kind of daze as I move around the tiny basement flat trying to make sense of the chaos. It's like digging through the rubble of a bombed museum. Everywhere I turn I see evidence of the life my father once had, a life I can barely remember living with him. But among his things there isn't a single bottle of booze or beer can. I'm almost disappointed, vaguely alarmed. When my mother comes to pick me up at his building after a day of cleaning, I tell her that I think he'd finally stopped drinking. I'm painfully aware I wouldn't have believed it from him.

A few months later I rent the movie *Leaving Las Vegas*. I settle in to watch Nicholas Cage's character drink himself to death, working my way through a two-four of beer as I lament my father's early demise. There is something thrilling about this night, something dark and sad and thrilling. A sick but sweet sense of communion with my father arises.

Without being conscious of it, I begin to drink differently. I tell myself it is my father's darkness I need to understand. Night after night, I drink in the room where I keep my father's ashes, believing we are getting to know each other at last. The real us: losers both. I know it is only a matter of time before people figure out that, despite my wisecracking exterior and seeming strength, I am my father's daughter. Frightened of everything, incapable of shrugging off the smallest disappointments, I listen to music and drink. I watch late movies and drink some more. On the nights I stand in crowded bars with friends, my thoughts are on getting back to the six-pack I've stashed in my fridge for later. I meet a version of myself I'd sworn would never exist, a pathetic creature whose survival quietly depends on cans and bottles.

My father died in March of 1996. One morning in October 1999 I sit with my face in my hands, my head pounding from a hangover. I sit as I have on so many mornings after, wondering how and when my life became so small and dark. If this is what being an adult is all about, I think, I'd rather die. The thought startles me. I realize I can no longer continue to maintain the grand façade I grew up with: Everything is fine. Or, if it's not fine today, hell, there's always tomorrow! I look in the mirror and know that I'm a pretty dubious example of what fine looks like. Things that once gave me pleasure have ceased to do so, one by one. Who cared about getting up at sunrise anyway? Who needed stacks of clean clothes piled neatly in drawers? But the fear that I might lose my desire to do the one thing that gives me happiness—writing—sends a shudder through me. No, I think, not my words, they're all I can count on. Plenty of writers drink a lot and continue to write books—sometimes even great ones—but something in me knows I'm not up for that sort of struggle. I've tried, and it isn't working.

When I find myself sitting in a church basement surrounded by self-professed alcoholics, all I can think about is my father. I hate him for his bad example; I feel he has driven me to the same awful place. At the same time I wonder if I really need to be there. Maybe I'm just paranoid or a little undisciplined. Maybe I could still drink occasionally. I've walked into the meeting thinking that my pain is unique, that no one here will have anything to teach me because I'm an artist with a "special" set of problems. But my awareness of my father's inability to reach outside himself keeps my ass firmly planted on a folding chair when all I want to do is run. He chose to drown; I want to swim. I want a hell of a lot from life for as long as I'm meant to have it. As I listen to the people around me talk about their drinking, I know that I too am going to need some help. For the first time in my life, I ask for it.

Now, two years later, my deepest sources of strength and inspiration come not from meetings, labels or counting the number of days lived without alcohol but from writing, reading and being with friends. I've never told myself I won't *ever* have a drink again, but that, for today, I'll probably choose not to. I concentrate on how wonderful it will be to get up early with a clear head and a quiet courage I didn't know I possessed. This version of me is the one I like best so far, the one who knows she is no worse (and no better) than anyone else, her father included.

It would be great to be able to say I drank too much because my father did. It would be easy to say I drank too often because I'm a writer, and that's what real writers do. But now I think my drinking got out of control because *I wanted it to.* Initially, booze gave me an outlet, a kind of comfort I couldn't find anywhere else. But as time went on, alcohol made me more afraid, not less. The answer to my lifelong questions about my father's drinking didn't come zooming into focus as I had hoped they would. His reasons were his reasons, and I will never know what they were. I'd be lying if I said I'm not furious and heartbroken that he isn't here now, when I've learned what I have about being alive, about drinking and drowning and all the rest of it. I wish we could have known each other as adults. But the truth is, it took his death to teach me how not to live my life. I guess that's the ultimate gift of my father's bad example, and though it's taken me years, I accept it—with both hands.

In memory of my father and for my mom, who believes in swimming.

GRAND THEFTS

TOM BISSELL

ONCE UPON A time I wrote in the morning, jogged in the late afternoon and spent most of my evenings reading. Once upon a time I wrote off as unproductive those days in which I had managed to put down "only" a thousand words. Once upon a time I played videogames almost exclusively with friends. Once upon a time I did occasionally binge on games, but these binges rarely had less than a fortnight between them. Once upon a time I was, more or less, content.

"Once upon a time" refers to relatively recent years (2001–2006), during which I wrote several books and published more than 50 pieces of magazine journalism and criticism—a total output of, give or take, 4,500 manuscript pages. I rarely felt very disciplined during this half decade, though I realize this admission invites accusations of disingenuousness. Obviously I *was* disciplined. These days I have read from start to finish exactly two works of fiction—excepting those I was also reviewing—in the last year. These days I play video games in the morning, play video games in the afternoon and spend my evenings playing video games. These days I still manage to write, but the times I am able to do so for more than three sustained hours have the temporal periodicity of comets with near-Earth trajectories.

For a while I hoped that my inability to concentrate on writing and reading was the result of a charred and overworked thalamus. I knew the pace I was on was not sustainable and figured my discipline was treating itself to a rumspringa. I waited patiently for it to stroll back onto the farm, apologetic but invigorated. When this did not happen, I wondered if my intensified attraction to games and my desensitized attraction to literature were reasonable responses to how formally compelling games had quite suddenly become. Three years into my predicament, my discipline remains AWOL. Games, meanwhile, are even more formally compelling.

It has not helped that during the past three years I have, for what seemed like compelling reasons at the time, frequently upended my life, moving from New York City to Rome to Las Vegas to Tallinn, Estonia, and back, finally, to the United States. With every move I resolved to leave behind my video game consoles, counting on new surroundings, unfamiliar people and different cultures to enable a rediscovery of the joy I once took in my work. Shortly after arriving in Rome, Las Vegas and Tallinn, however, the lines of gameless resolve I had chalked across my mind were wiped clean. In Rome this took two months; in Vegas two weeks; in Tallinn two days. Thus I enjoy the spendthrift distinction of having purchased four Xbox 360 consoles in three years, having abandoned the first to the care of a friend in Brooklyn, left another floating around Europe with parties unknown, and stranded another with a pal in Tallinn (to the irritation of his girlfriend). The last Xbox 360 I bought has plenty of companions: a GameCube, a PlayStation 2 and a PlayStation 3.

Writing and reading allow one consciousness to find and take shelter in another. When the minds of the reader and writer perfectly and inimitably connect, objects, events and emotions become doubly vivid—more real, somehow, than real things. I have spent most of my life seeking out these connections and attempting to create my own. Today, however, the pleasures of literary connection seem leftover and familiar. Today the most consistently pleasurable pursuit in my life is playing video games. Unfortunately, the least useful and financially solvent pursuit in my life is also playing video games. For instance, I woke up this morning at 8 AM fully intending to write this article. Instead, I played *Left 4 Dead* until 5 PM. The rest of the day went up in a blaze of intermittent catnaps. It is now 10 PM and I have only just started to work. I know how I will spend the late, frayed moments before I go to sleep tonight, because they are how I spent last night and the night before that: walking the perimeter of my empty bed and carpet-bombing the equally empty bedroom with promises that tomorrow will not be squandered. I will fall asleep in a futureless, strangely peaceful panic, not really knowing what I will do the next morning and having no firm memory of who, or what, I once was.

The first video game I can recall having to force myself to stop playing was Rockstar's *Grand Theft Auto: Vice City*, which was released in 2002. I managed to miss *Vice City*'s storied predecessor, *Grand Theft Auto III*, so I had only oblique notions of what I was getting into. A friend had lobbied me to buy *Vice City*, so I knew its basic premise: you are a cold-blooded jailbird looking to ascend the bloody social ladder of the fictional Vice City's criminal under- and overworld. (I also knew that Vice City's violent subject matter was said to have inspired crime sprees by a few of the game's least stable fans. Other such sprees would horribly follow. Eight years later, Rockstar has spent more time in court than a playground-abutting pesticide manufactory.) I might have taken better note of the fact that my friend, when speaking of *Vice City*, admitted he had not slept more than four hours a night since purchasing it and had the ocular spasms and fuse-blown motor reflexes to prove it. Just what, I wanted to know, was so specifically compelling about *Vice City*? "Just get it and play it," he answered. "You can do anything you want in the game. Anything."

My friend's promise proved to be an exaggeration but not by very much. You control a young man named Tommy, who has been recently released from prison. He arrives in Vice City—an oceanside metropolis obviously modelled on the Miami of 1986 or so—only to be double-crossed during a coke deal. A few minutes into the game, you watch a cut scene in which Tommy and his lawyer (an anti-Semitic parody of an anti-Semitic parody) decide that revenge must be taken and the coke recovered. Once the cut scene ends, you step outside your lawyer's office. A car is waiting for you. You climb in and begin your drive to the mission destination (a clothing store) clearly marked on your map. The first thing you notice is that your car's radio can be tuned to a number of different radio stations. What is playing on these stations is not a loop of upbeat midi video-game songs or some bombastic score written for the game, but Michael Jackson, Hall & Oates, Cutting Crew and Luther Vandross. While you are wondering at this, you hop a curb, run over some pedestrians and slam into a parked car, all of which a nearby police officer sees. He promptly gives chase. And for the first time you are off, speeding through Vice City's various neighbourhoods. You are still getting accustomed to the driving controls and come into frequent contact with jaywalkers, oncoming traffic, streetlights, fire hydrants. Soon your pummelled car (you shed your driver's door two blocks ago) is smoking.

The police, meanwhile, are still in pursuit. You dump the dying car and start to run. How do you get another car? As it happens, a sleek little sporty number called the Stinger is idling beneath a stoplight right in front of you. This game is called *Grand Theft Auto*, is it not? You approach the car, hit the assigned button and watch Tommy rip the owner from the vehicle, throw him onto the street and drive off. Wait—look there! A motorcycle. Can you drive motorcycles, too? After another brutal vehicular jacking, you fly off an angled ramp in cinematic slow motion while ELO's "Four Little Diamonds" strains the limits of your television's pound-coin-sized speakers.

You have now lost the cops and swing around to head back to your mission, the purpose of which you have forgotten. It gradually dawns on you that this mission is waiting for you to reach it. You do not have to go if you do not want to. Feeling liberated, you drive around Vice City as day gives way to night. When you finally hop off the bike, the citizens of Vice City mumble and yell insults. You approach a man in a construction worker's outfit. He stops, looks at you and waits. The game does not give you any way to interact with this man other than through physical violence, so you take a swing. The fight ends with you stomping the last remaining vitality from the hapless construction worker's blood-squirting body.

When you finally decide to return to the mission point, the rhythm of the game is established. Exploration, mission, cut scene, driving, mayhem, success, exploration, mission, cut scene, driving, mayhem, success. Never has a game felt so open. Never has a game felt so generationally relevant. Never has a game felt so awesomely gratuitous. Never has a game felt so narcotic. When you stopped playing *Vice City*, its leash-snapped world somehow seemed to go on without you.

Vice City's sequel, *Grand Theft Auto: San Andreas*, was several magnitudes larger—so large, in fact, I never finished the game. *San Andreas* gave gamers not one city to explore but three, all of them set in the hip-hop demimonde of California in the early 1990s (though one of the cities is a Vegas clone). It also added dozens of diversions, the most needless of which was the ability of your controlled character, a young man named C.J., to get fat from eating health-restoring pizza and burgers—fat that could be burned off only by hauling C.J.'s porky ass down to the gym to ride a stationary bike and lift weights. This resulted in a lot of soul-scouring questions as to why a) it even mattered to me that C.J. was fat and why b) C.J. was getting more physical exercise than I was. Because I could not answer either question satisfactorily, I stopped playing.

Grand Theft Auto IV was announced in May 2006, six months after the launch of the Xbox 360 and six months before the launch of the PlayStation 3, the "next-generation" platforms that have since pushed gaming into the cultural mainstream. When the first next-gen titles began to appear, it was clear that the previous *Grand Theft Auto* titles—much like Hideo Kojima's similarly brilliant and similarly frustrated *Metal Gear Solid* titles—were games of next-gen vision and ambition without next-gen hardware to support them. The early word was that *GTA IV* would scale back the excesses of San Andreas and provide a rounder, more succinctly inhabited game experience. I was living in Las Vegas when *GTA IV* (after a heartbreaking six-month delay) was finally released.

In Vegas I had made a friend who shared my sacramental devotion to marijuana, my dilated obsession with gaming and my ballistic impatience to play *GTA IV*. When I was walking home from my neighbourhood game store with my reserved copy of *GTA IV* in hand, I called my friend to tell him. He let me know that, to celebrate the occasion, he was bringing over some "extra sweetener." My friend's taste in recreational drug abuse vastly exceeded my own, and this extra sweetener turned out to be an alarming quantity of cocaine, a substance with which I had one prior and unexpectedly amiable experience, though I had not seen a frangible white nugget of the stuff since.

While the *GTA IV* load screen appeared on my television screen, my friend chopped up a dozen lines, reminded me of basic snorting protocol and handed me the straw. I hesitated before taking the tiny hollow sceptre but not for too long. Know this: I was not someone whose life had been marked by the meticulous collection of bad habits. I chewed tobacco, regularly drank about ten Diet Cokes a day, and liked marijuana. Beyond that, my greatest vice was probably reading poetry for pleasure. The coke sailed up my nasal passage, leaving behind the delicious smell of a hot leather car seat on the way back from the beach. My previous coke experience had made feeling good an emergency, but this was something else, softer and almost relaxing. This coke, my friend told me, had not been "stepped on" with any amphetamine, and I pretended to know what that meant. I felt as intensely focused as a diamond-cutting laser; *Grand Theft Auto IV* was ready to go. My friend and I played it for the next thirty hours straight.

Many children who want to believe their tastes are adult will bravely try coffee, find it to be undeniably awful but recognize something that could one day, conceivably, be enjoyed. Once our tastes as adults are fully developed, it is easy to forget the effort that went into them. Adult taste can be demanding work—so hard, in fact, that some of us, when we become adults, selectively take up a few childish things, as though in defeated acknowledgement that adult taste, with its many bewilderments, is frequently more trouble than it is worth. Few games have more to tell us about this adult retreat into childishness than the *Grand Theft Auto* series.

In *GTA IV* you are Niko Bellic, a young immigrant with an ambiguous past. We know he is probably a Serb. We know he fought in the Balkan Wars. We know he was party to a war-crime atrocity and victim of a double-cross that led to the slaughter of all but three members of his paramilitary unit. We know he has taken life outside of war, and it is strongly suggested that he once dabbled in human trafficking. "I did some dumb things and got involved with some idiots," Niko says, early in the game, to his friend Hassan. "We all do dumb things," Hassan replies. "That's what makes us human." The camera closes on Niko as he thinks about this, and for a moment his face becomes as quietly expressive as that of a living actor. "Could be," he says.

Niko has come to Liberty City (the *GTA* world's run at New York City) at the invitation of his prevaricating cousin, Roman. He wants to start over, leave behind the death and madness of his troubled past, and bathe in the comfort and safety of America. Niko's plan does not go well. Soon enough he is working as a thief and killer. Just as *Lolita*, as Nabokov piquantly notes in his afterword, was variously read as "old Europe debauching young America" or "young America debauching old Europe," *GTA IV* leaves itself interpretatively open as to whether Niko is corrupted by America or whether he and his ilk (many of the most vicious characters whose paths Niko crosses are immigrants) are themselves bacterial agents of corruption. The earlier *GTA* games were less thematically ambitious. Tommy from *Vice City* is a cackling psychopath, and C.J. from *San Andreas* merely rides the acquisitionist philosophy of hip-hop culture to terminal amorality. They are not characters you root for or even want, in moral terms, to succeed. You want them to succeed only in gameplay terms. The better they do, the more of the gameworld you see.

The stories in *Vice City* and *San Andreas* are pastiches of tired filmic genres: crime capers, ghetto dramas, police procedurals. The driving force of both games is the gamer's curiosity: *What happens next? What is over here? What if I do this?* They are, in this way, childlike and often very silly games, especially *San Andreas*, which lets you cover your body with ridiculous tattoos and even fly a jetpack. While the gameworlds and subject matter are adult—and under no circumstances should children be allowed near either game—the joy of the gameplay is allowing the vestiges of a repressed, tantrum-throwing, childlike self to run amok. Most games are about attacking a childlike world with an adult mind. The *GTA* games are the opposite, and one of the most maliciously entertaining mini-games in *Vice City* and *San Andreas* is a mayhem mode in which the only goal is to fuck up as much of the gameworld as possible in an allotted period of time.

Niko's real pathos derives not from the gimcrack story but how he looks and moves. *Vice City* and *San Andreas* were graphically astounding by the standards of their time, but their character models were woeful—even by the standards of their time. Niko, though, is just about perfect. Dressed in striped black track pants and a dirty windbreaker, Niko looked like the kind of guy one might see staring longingly at the entrance of a strip club in Zagreb, too poor to get in and too self-conscious to try to. When, early in the game, a foul-mouthed minor Russian mafioso named Vlad dismisses Niko as a "yokel," he is not wrong. Niko is a yokel, pathetically so. One of the first things you have to do as Niko is buy new clothes in a Broker (read: Brooklyn) neighbourhood called Hove Beach (read: Sheepshead Bay). The clothing store in question is Russian-owned, its wares fascinatingly ugly. And yet you know, somehow, that Niko, with his slightly less awful new clothes, feels as though he is moving up in the world. The fact that he is only makes him more heartrending. The times I identified most with Niko were not during the game's frequent cut scenes, which drop bombs of "meaning" and "narrative importance" with nuclear delicacy, but rather when I watched him move through the world of Liberty City and projected onto him my own guesses as to what he was thinking and feeling.

What many without direct experience of the games do know is that they allow you to kill police officers. This is true. *GTA* games also allow you to kill everyone else. It is sometimes assumed that you somehow get points for killing police officers. Of course you do not get "points" for anything in *GTA IV*. You get money for completing missions, a number of which are, yes, monstrously violent. While the passersby and pedestrians you slay out of mission will occasionally drop money, it would be hard to argue that the game rewards you for indiscriminate slaughter. People never drop that much money, for one, and the best way to attract the attention of the police and begin a hair-raising transborough chase is to hurt an innocent person. As for the infamous cultural trope that in *GTA* you can hire a prostitute, pay her, kill her and take her money, this is also true. But you do not have to do this. The game certainly does not ask you to do this. Indeed, after being serviced by a prostitute, Niko will often say something like: "Strange. All that effort to feel this empty." Outside of the inarguably violent missions, it is not what *GTA IV* asks you to do that is so morally alarming. It is what it allows you to do.

There is no question, though, that *GTA IV*'s violence can be extremely disturbing, because it feels unprecedentedly distinct from how, say, films deal with violence. Think of the scene in *Goodfellas* in which Henry, Tommy and Jimmy kick to death Billy Batts in Henry's restaurant. Afterwards they decide to put Batts's body in the trunk of Henry's car and bury it in the forest. Of course Batts is not yet dead and spends much of the ride to his place of interment weakly banging the trunk's interior. When Batts is discovered to be alive he is repeatedly, nightmarishly stabbed. The viewer of *Goodfellas* is implicated in the fate of Billy Batts in any number of ways. Most of us presumably feel closest to Henry, who has the least to do with the crime but is absolutely an accomplice to it. Henry's point of view is our implied point of view. Thus we/Henry, unlike Tommy and Jimmy, retain our capacity for horror.

In *GTA IV*, Niko is charged with disposing of the bodies of two men whose deaths Niko is partially responsible for. You/Niko drive across Liberty City with these bodies in the trunk to a corrupt physician who plans to sell the organs on the black market. Here the horror of the situation is refracted in an entirely different manner, which allows the understanding that *GTA IV* is an engine of a far more intimate process of implication. While on his foul errand, Niko must cope with lifelike traffic, police harassment, red lights, pedestrians and a poorly handling loan car. Literally thousands of in-game variables complicate what you are trying to do. The *Goodfellas* scene is an observed experience bound up in one's own moral perception. The *GTA IV* mission is a procedural event in which one's moral perception of the (admittedly much sillier) situation is scrambled by myriad other distractions. It turns narrative into an active experience, which film is simply unable to do in the same way. And it is moments like this that remind me why I love video games and what they give me that nothing else can.

"Cocaine," Robert Sabbag tells us in the smuggling classic *Snowblind*, "has no edge. It is strictly a motor drug. It does not alter your perception; it will not even wire you up like the amphetamines. No pictures, no time/space warping, no danger, no fun, no edge. Any individual serious about his chemicals—a heavy hitter—would sooner take 30 No-Doz [caffeine tablets]. Coke is to acid what jazz is to rock. You have to appreciate it. *It* does not come to *you.*"

Cocaine has its reputation as aggression unleaded largely because many who are attracted to it are themselves aggressive personalities, the reasons for which are as cultural as they are financial. What cocaine does is italicize personality traits, not script new ones. In my case, cocaine did not heighten my aggression in the least. What it did, at least at first, was exaggerate my natural curiosity and need for emotional affection. While on cocaine I became as harmlessly ravenous as Cookie Monster.

This stage, lamentably and predictably, did not last long. A large portion of my last two months in Las Vegas was spent doing cocaine and playing video games—usually *Grand Theft Auto IV*. When I left Vegas, I thought I was leaving behind not only video games but cocaine. During the last walk I took through the city, in May 2008, I imagined the day's heat as the whoosh of a bullet that, through some oversight of fate, I had managed to dodge. (I was on cocaine at the time.) Even though one of the first things I did when I arrived in Tallinn was buy yet another Xbox 360, I had every intention to obey one of my few prime directives: rigorous adherence to all foreign drug laws. I had been in Tallinn for five months when, in a club, I found myself chatting with someone who was obviously lit. When I gently indicated my awareness of this person's altered state, the result was a magnanimous offer to share. Within no time at all I was back in my apartment, high on cocaine and firing up my Xbox 360. By the week's end, I had a new friend, a new telephone number and a reignited habit. I played through *Grand Theft Auto IV* again and again after that. The game was faster and more beautiful while I was on cocaine, and breaking laws seemed even more seductive. Niko and I were outlaws, alone as all outlaws are alone, but deludedly content with our freedom and our power.

Soon I was sleeping in my clothes. Soon my hair was stiff and fragrantly unclean. Soon I was doing lines before my Estonian class, staying up for days, curating prodigious nosebleeds and spontaneously vomiting from exhaustion. Soon my pillowcases bore rusty coins of nasal drippage. Soon the only thing I could smell was something like the inside of an empty bottle of prescription medicine. Soon my biweekly phone call to my cocaine dealer was a weekly phone call. Soon I was walking into the night, handing hundreds of dollars in cash to a Russian man whose name I did not even know, waiting in alleys for him to come back—which he always did, though I never fully expected him to—and retreating home, to my Xbox, to *GTA IV*, to the electrifying solitude of my mind at play in an anarchic digital world. Soon I began to wonder why the only thing I seemed to like to do while on cocaine was play video games. And soon I realized what video games have in common with cocaine: video games, you see, have no edge. You have to appreciate them. They do not come to you.

There are times when I think *GTA IV* is the most colossal creative achievement of the last twenty-five years, times when I think of it as an unsurpassable example of what games can do, and times when I think of it as misguided and a failure. No matter what I think about *GTA IV*, or however I am currently regarding it, my throat gets a little drier, my head a little heavier, and I know I am also thinking about cocaine.

Video games and cocaine feed on my impulsiveness, reinforce my love of solitude and make me feel good and bad in equal measure. The crucial difference is that I believe in what video games want to give me, while the bequest of cocaine is one I loathe. I do know that video games have enriched my life. Of that I have no doubt. They have also done damage to my life. Of that I have no doubt. I let this happen, of course; I even helped the process along. As for cocaine, it has been a long time since I last did it but not as long as I would like.

What have games given me? Experiences. Not surrogate experiences but actual experiences, many of which are as important to me as any real memories. Once I wanted games to show me things I could not see in any other medium. Then I wanted games to tell me a story in a way no other medium can. Then I wanted games to redeem something absent in myself. Then I wanted a game experience that pointed not toward but at something. Playing *GTA IV* on coke for weeks and then months at a time, I learned that maybe all a game can do is point at the person who is playing it, and maybe this has to be enough.

I still have an occasional thought about Niko. When I last left him he was trying to find all the super jump cheats hidden around Liberty City, which is a strange thing for a wanted fugitive to be doing. I know he is still there, in his dingy South Bohan apartment, waiting for me to rejoin him. In early 2009, Rockstar released some new downloadable content for *GTA IV*, *The Lost and Damned*, in which you follow the narrative path of Johnny Klebitz, an incidental character in Niko's story (his most memorable line: "Nothing like selling a little dope to let you know you're alive!"), but whose story, it turns out, intersects with Niko's in interesting ways. I played this new *GTA IV* story for a few hours but gradually lost interest and finally gave up. I realized, dismayingly, that a lot of what powered me through *GTA IV* had been the cocaine, though it is still my favourite game and probably always will be. I was no longer the person I had been when I loved *GTA IV* the most, and without Niko Liberty City was not the same.

Niko was not my friend, but I felt for him, deeply. He was clearly having a hard go of it and did not always understand why. He was in a new place that did not make a lot of sense. He was trying, he was doing his best, but he was falling into habits and ways of being that did not reflect his best self. By the end of his long journey, Niko and I had been through a lot together.

JUNKIE GROWS UP

MOLLY JONG-FAST

DURING THE SUMMER of 1994, as part of the American government's Just Say No antidrug campaign, the television networks aired a public service spot that showed a ballerina stumbling while attempting a pirouette. A voice-over pronounced glumly, "No one ever says that when they grow up they want to be a junkie." The ballerina then fell to the floor in a cloud of pink tulle and apparent drug addiction.

My friends and I thought this ad was the most hilarious and naive piece of propaganda we had ever seen. Over the next four years, whenever the joke struck them, my friends would break into a chant: "No one ever says that when they grow up they want to be a junkie—except Molly Jong-Fast." And they were not wrong.

As far back as I could remember, I had dreamt of being a heroin addict. I wanted to have a secret life, to cavort with a bad element. I longed to be sickly, with dark circles under my eyes. I wanted to be worried about. I idolized Gia Carangi, the Cindy Crawford of the late seventies and the model who made heroin chic so glamorous before her death from AIDS in 1986. I loved *Drugstore Cowboy*, a dark movie starring the stunning Matt Dillon in a story about junkies who rob drugstores, and I fell half in love with easeful death. I imagined the folds between my toes concealing track marks. I fantasized that I would be found OD'd in a musty hotel room and rushed to the hospital. Then everyone would be sorry they hadn't been nicer to me.

Junkie-hood seemed to offer the antidote to being a fat teenager. (I also wanted to be as skinny as Calista Flockhart, pre-Harrison Ford.) As a child, I was always picked last, constantly humiliated, and repeatedly shamed about my lack of willpower. But as a drug addict, I could be an outsider and "cool" at the same time. As a junkie, I could be beautiful yet still show my suffering. The drugs would protect me from rejection, from the embarrassment of being overweight. And they could dull the painful notoriety of my publicly fractured family, a novelist mother and a screenwriter father who fought each other viciously for the right not to raise me.

Because of their peculiar disinterest, I understood that there could be a moment when my parents would cut me off entirely, when they decided that I was just too much work for too little return. It might be okay to sniff glue until you saw stars or snort cocaine and sleep with some blank-faced guy old enough to be your father, but it was not okay to become a hooker or get pregnant in high school. That would be crossing the demarcation line into cautionary tale. A few years of youthful indiscretion were allowed, but eventually I had to do the things normal middle-class children did, like graduate from college.

I had known rich private-school kids who had fallen off the edge. Being disowned or cut off wasn't as unlikely as it seemed. Two high-school acquaintances had killed themselves with drugs—it's impossible to know whether they wanted to die or it was just a mistake with the doses—and another had ended up in the world of food stamps and public assistance. I knew how it went: begging for money from rich relatives, couch surfing with friends in SoHo, and then finding that family members pretended not to know you when you passed them on the street. Parental love on Park Avenue is more conditional than you might think.

Heroin is ultimately about suicide—passive, lazy, enjoyable self-destruction—yet suicide isn't in my blood. Sure, there's a sketchy family history of alcoholism, including a grandmother who knocked back six shots of vodka every night, but my family isn't like the Vanderbilts, one of those clans for whom suicide is as common a cause of death as cancer. Perhaps Jews are less partial to suicide, thanks to centuries of anti-Semitism, pogroms, and annihilation at the hands of others. History has tempered my people's self-destructive impulses.

Still, I tested that theory. By the fall of 1997, I was a nineteen-year-old with a double deviated septum that was as soft as cream cheese and ready to collapse. I was snorting an eight-ball of cocaine every day. I was ingesting six to ten Klonopins, a Valium-like drug, every twenty-four hours. I was drinking beer and vodka. I was known as my then-boyfriend's "junkie girlfriend." (He was a drug user, too, and a troublemaker, but clearly more functional than I was.)

I thought vodka and Klonopin went together like milk and cookies. I thought no one had ever died from inhaling too much cocaine. Of course I was also sure that beer wasn't alcohol and Tylenol could be consumed like M&Ms. Thin at last from the cocaine, I ate little more than frozen yogurt and sprinkles, those multi-coloured specks of sugar that were, ironically, the happiest accessories of my weirdly permissive, weirdly pathetic childhood.

On October 30, after another night of cocaine and Corona followed by the awful coming down that could only be tempered by a huge amount of Valium, I wandered the Upper West Side, stoned out of my mind, hoping to be hit by a car. I stopped in front of my grandparents' apartment on Central Park West. I wanted to go in, see them and talk to them, but I was too much of a mess to get past their hawk-eyed doorman.

It was that small realization, and the shame that came with it, that tipped everything, that made me call my shrink for help. She immediately directed me to an addiction specialist. The specialist told me that I needed to go away, and I agreed. My preference was the Betty Ford Center; there would be celebrities everywhere. But he convinced me that the Hazelden rehab centre in Minnesota had sheltered its share of celebrities too, so Hazelden it was. I hoped Elizabeth Taylor might be my roommate.

My mother and I flew to Minnesota on Northwest Airlines, on November 1, 1997. I checked seven pieces of Prada luggage, all filled with designer clothing. In the departure lounge, my mother begged me to take only one Klonopin, but when she turned her back, I downed four. On the plane I drank four glasses of white wine and soon passed out. When we landed, I took a long look at the icy tundra and reconsidered suicide as an escape route. Suddenly this rehab thing seemed significantly less fun than in the movies.

We were met by an elderly woman who drove us to Hazelden in an old station wagon—not quite the limousine with tinted windows I had hoped for—through a dark and snow-covered landscape dotted with ice houses, signs for towns with Norwegian names, and countless liquor stores. Writer Rob Bingham's description of Minnesota in his book *Pure Slaughter Value* captured its freakishness perfectly. He wrote about a bar that traded a Hazelden medallion—an Alcoholics Anonymous reward for staying sober—for a free drink. Bingham must have known what that bar at the end of the world looked like; he died of a heroin overdose at the age of thirty-three. Before then, he had been a frequent visitor to Hazelden.

When we arrived, a nurse searched my bags for drugs and confiscated my giant bottle of Klonopin. I explained that I needed it for anxiety, that she should call my shrink. She was unmoved; she said she had already talked to my shrink. After a twenty-minute argument, she gave me a paper cup of meds—weak withdrawal medicine—and I went to bed under a polyester comforter.

I was the sickest patient on the detox unit, so they put me in a corner room, one equipped with oxygen tanks. Every fifteen minutes there was a quiet click of the door as a friendly nurse padded in, leaned over me, and took my blood pressure. Sometimes it was ninety over seventy, sometimes it was lower. That first night I had horrible nightmares. In the morning, my window panes were covered by thick, white frost. Click, click went the door, and I thought I saw someone I used to know. Click, click, and I longed for it to lock for good.

I was proud that my condition required two more days than most in detox. My mother called constantly. I tried to get her secretary to send me a plane ticket home. By that point, I was feeling better and thought maybe this was all a mistake.

After four days on the detox ward, I was moved to Lily, one of Hazelden's two wards for women. The other patients despised me. I wore my Prada coat and smoked cigarettes. I bragged about my notorious mother and my parents' money. I boasted about my well-connected boyfriend and the meaningless parties I attended. The truth is I bragged to prop myself up, to cover an ego crippled by self-loathing. My dignity had long since been dissolved by promiscuity, by stealing, by lying, by shaming myself in a million different ways.

My counsellor was a grey-haired woman named Patty who had a Minnesota drawl, sad eyes, a very soft voice, and an office filled with stuffed animals and platitude-covered posters. She claimed she had shot cocaine, but I didn't really buy it. I thought she must hate me. Often I would sit in the chair at her desk and cry about how my mother had never loved me, feeling profoundly sorry for myself. Sometimes Patty would smile and humour me; sometimes she would challenge me, and when she did, I hated her.

After three weeks, I had submitted to my assigned chores and conscientious vacuuming had earned me the privilege of my own room. I had given up the façade of not being an alcoholic. The other girls became friendlier, and I became a member of the community, almost an old-timer. One night, a few of us were smoking out on the porch. The air was so cold we could see our breath, but we had just ordered an enormous Carvel ice cream cake.

"You know," said an older woman with silver hair and yellowed teeth, "I went to my first rehab at nineteen." She smiled and exhaled a puff of smoke in my direction.

"I was twenty," another sighed.

"I was fifteen," an obese woman added.

"I was twenty-one," said a woman whose face was covered in methamphetamine sores.

It occurred to me in that moment that rehabilitation could become an occupation for me. I could be in and out of rehab, drinking and not drinking, for the rest of my ever-diminishing days. I had been so consumed with myself, with preserving a front, with the idea that rehab was a personal failure, that I had never really understood that my life was at stake. Sooner rather than later, I was going to overdose and die or drink myself to death. That night, in the cold Minnesota air, I got sober.

I spent Thanksgiving of 1997 at Hazelden. My mother and father and stepmother and stepfather all came out to be with me. We ate a delicious turkey dinner on plastic plates—the food at Hazelden was fantastic, it must be said—and afterwards we walked around the elegantly landscaped grounds. I was still a patient and I could not leave, but it was my best Thanksgiving ever. When I got home in early December, I started going to twelve-step meetings and seeing a therapist who specialized in addiction.

As I write this, I have been sober for eight years. I was sober—drug-free and alcohol-free—for my twenty-first birthday, for the birth of my first child, on my wedding day, and at the deaths of my two grandfathers. I have been sober longer than not, but that's meaningless. I could drink a bottle or snort a line tomorrow. I could be on a plane back to Hazelden the day after or, worse, drunk but not on that plane. I am the kind of person who relapses, and that's why I must attend a twelve-step meeting every day, no matter how many clean years I can claim, and why I remind myself frequently that I am sober only by the grace of God. It's a mantra, and it works.

Most people who attempt rehabilitation will nonetheless die drunk or wasted. Within days of my departure from Hazelden, actor Chris Farley checked in. Not long after he left, he was found dead, overdosed on a speedball. A woman who became an AA "sponsee" of mine died of acute pancreatitis when she was only thirty-nine. She had famous parents and a big apartment on Central Park West and I was sure she'd get it in the way that I'd got it: that the effort is every day, for today. But she never did, never put together more than three sober months, never thought that an affluent, well-educated person could kill herself with alcohol.

I don't know why some people survive and others don't. Sobriety, like snowflakes and sprinkles and everything else wonderful in life, is oddly ethereal. But I do know that there is no glamour in alcoholism or drug addiction, no romance in dying of either, and that as long as I am alive, I will always struggle against both.

AN OPEN LETTER TO LAURA

LOIS SIMMIE

So you've reached the Crunch. I always think of it that way, that horrible place where you know you can't drink any more and you can't not drink. It's different from the annual New Year's resolutions, or those hideously hung-over declarations that made us feel so virtuous. For a while. I stopped so many times it got embarrassing. "Are you on or off the wagon?" friends would ask, and usually I fell off in the time it took to ask the question. The Crunch. The alcoholic Big C. It's the end of the road. You know.

You've been to your first meeting of sober alcoholics, seen the faces, heard the stories. Like me at my first meeting, you were amazed that we looked so good, could laugh at ourselves, but if we only dwelled on the bad stuff there'd be no one there. And absurd things happened to alcoholics, of course. A natural-born klutz, I fell up and down stairs, in and out of cars, *under* one twice. I guess I wasn't meant to die of carbon monoxide poisoning. Or alcoholism, thank God. And neither are you.

You told us you want to stay sober more than anything. More than you want to drink, you said, and then added "almost," and everyone laughed. But that's the place we need to get to or it isn't going to happen. Hold that resolve close, Laura. Make it your mantra against the times when you're sorely tempted. You want to stay sober more than you want to drink.

As for the nitty-gritty, when your gut is tied in that knot that only a drink can fix? When a meeting is hours away, and no one answers the phone? Then you don't drink an hour at a time, a few minutes even, *just till this damn craving passes and I can think!* That long. Take deep breaths. (I'd have killed without my cigarettes.) Drink anything but booze till you slosh. Get out and walk, maybe to the library; they never offer you drinks there. And when that urge passes, quit for another hour. You're trying to save your life. Not that the grim prospect of insanity, cirrhosis or death ever stopped an alcoholic. *(Hey, it was a good liver while it lasted.)* It's the sickness of the soul that gets us.

You're heartsick about what you're doing to your children. That's sobered up more women alcoholics than anything else, I think. We love our children, and most of us didn't beat our kids, weren't maliciously cruel. We didn't break bones, we broke promises. That movie they looked forward to, but friends dropped by and we poured drinks and it was "We'll go next week, okay, honey?" And they can't say it damn well isn't okay. Or we were sick with "the flu"—that malevolent virus that unfairly attacked us more than other people—and couldn't have survived all those screaming kids at the swimming pool, doing well if we managed to get out of bed in time to make supper. Or we missed a parent-teacher interview with that same strain of flu.

But now we have the chance to try to make it up to them. Unlike my old school friend, who wouldn't or couldn't be honest with herself long enough to stay stopped. The fifteen-year-old son she loved so much found her dead in bed, her liver destroyed by cirrhosis, her skin a shocking ochre. No open casket at that funeral. A cherished, *needed* mother, who couldn't call herself alcoholic, lost to alcohol. Your children will have a mother, Laura, not just the faint memory of a woman who cried as she hugged them too tight.

It was dread of what might happen to my children that brought me to the Crunch. Did I really drive 150 miles home from Regina after drinking all night, no sleep, at eighty-five, ninety miles an hour, waking up twice heading for the ditch, the ten-year-old son I adored asleep on the back seat? I shook all that day like never before. Like I might fly apart.

And, shortly after, the obscene phone call, *I'm going to fuck your daughter*, my wild drive out to the stables, frantic to find the one not at home. I sat on a hard bench and watched her fourteen-year-old grace as she rode around and around the ring, her hair, the horse's coat shining the same reddish blonde under the light. No one else there. Vulnerable. I recognized that voice on the phone. It was the man I'd invited to share our table at a dance the night before, my husband not impressed and who could blame him? Everybody was my best friend when I drank. I'd blabbed away to a total stranger: who we were, where we lived, the kids' activities, he was so interested in those. On the bench in that empty arena, I wept for what could have happened to her. For what had happened to me.

A week later I told the psychiatrist treating my depression that I thought I might have a drinking problem *(thought? might?)*, and he asked if I'd ever had a blackout. When I said, "Oh, yes" (like didn't *everybody?*), "Only alcoholics have blackouts," he informed me, and suggested where I could go for help. He looked so sorry for me. But I was elated. God, yes, I wasn't crazy! Not a bad person! Just an alcoholic! How bloody wonderful! And I still think so.

Alcoholics' stories are so similar, Laura, except for the details—my highway story; you driving drunk on a five-lane freeway to hockey practice, the kids too scared to squabble; Al telling about the flask in his briefcase that leaked all over a client's papers; your son hugging you and feeling the airline liquor bottles taped under your breasts. The young guy who came out of a blackout in another city to find his dead hamster packed in his suitcase. And my favourite, the haberdasher's son who'd thrown up, spilled wine, and fallen in the mud in an expensive wool suit and then, expecting a visit from Dad, put the suit through the washer and dryer at the laundromat. "It would have fit a monkey," he said. Stories sometimes hilarious, sometimes tragic, often moving. I'm hooked on the stories. I always have been.

The spouse who drinks too much is also familiar, and, yes, that will make it harder for you. Mine drank as much as I did, maybe more, losing his driver's licence at least twice, but he didn't call himself an alcoholic, and maybe he wasn't. He didn't suffer the guilt and remorse that became my almost constant companions, and to think I time and again invited their mean-spirited company tells you something about where I was in my life.

I'm grateful for those ghastly hangovers—the self-hatred, the bewilderment (I did it *again* in spite of my best intentions?), the awful inexplicable loneliness—that contributed to my final desperation. How can a woman sitting down as supper cooks, kids talking and playing around her, feel so alone? I didn't know that was a symptom of the illness. I loved it for so long: the warmth, the camaraderie, the silliness. "Pour me a drink, honey, it's already dark under the house." I couldn't believe it had turned mean, abusive, a love affair gone too wrong to save.

If your husband isn't happy losing his drinking partner—and some aren't—that's his problem, Laura. You won't have to remember the two of you shutting yourselves away in the den with a bottle to discuss your children's drug problems. That one still haunts me. I can see the printed burlap curtains in the bay window seat, the wall of books and the recliner chair I escaped into, the orange shag rug that popped up crumbs like fleas when raked. Can feel the hurt silence in the rest of the house. Those silences broke my heart. They still do as I write this. The marriage ended six years after I stopped drinking. We made so many mistakes. He put making a lot of money ahead of our troubled, mixed family, and I turned more and more to alcohol, until a comfort became a crutch became an illness. One that leaves scars.

As you learn about this disease—dis-ease so true in my case; I so often drank to feel comfortable—many things will fall into place. I saw the pile of self-help books on your coffee table last night. I read dozens of those books, one after another, especially when hungover, for the flicker of hope they sometimes offered. The truth was out there. The person I wanted to be. Had maybe even been before alcohol. The only trouble was, not one of those books mentioned alcohol; how it wastes so much time, holds you back. I had always planned to write, would often put down an indifferent novel and say "I sure as hell could write a better book than that," depressed deep down that I hadn't even tried. I never wrote a thing till I put away the rye and Coke (a sophisticated drinker I wasn't) for the last time. I have twelve books out there now, a new one this fall and a finished novel ready to go. You want to go to university, Laura, become a social worker. Now it's possible.

Christmas is almost here, and that's scary as hell. The year I finally stopped I planned to wait till after the festive season but only made it to December 15. Did I say festive? Driving the wrong way down a one-way street; lying naked on the bathroom floor all night too sick to leave the toilet; in bed after God knows how many drinks, a pack and a half of cigarettes and a couple of Valium to slow the motor, feeling my heart stop for what seemed like ages, oh God, was I going to die and ruin everybody's Christmas? As festive as gangrene creeping up your leg. The booze will be flowing, so give some thought to how you want to handle that. I always say "No thanks, it makes me drunk and disorderly." They think I'm kidding.

But how did I deal with *that* Christmas? With the visiting in-laws arguing about which house to buy; the niece in her terrible twos; the husband and brother-in-law emerging from the basement only to mix more drinks; loud drum rolls from the ten-year-old's new snare drum announcing arrivals, departures and everything else. (That kid, a journalist now with books of his own, proudly told his teachers about the secret club I'd joined for people who didn't drink.)

How did I get through it? By going to a meeting Christmas Eve; putting the turkey in the oven, grabbing my coat, and heading for one Christmas Day no matter what anybody thought; going to a meeting Boxing Day. And between meetings thinking about going to one. I can still remember the happy feeling that gave me. Thank God they're never cancelled. Someone is always there to open the doors, make the coffee, listen. Because every year there are white-knuckled people like me out there just hanging on till it's time for the meeting.

Early in my sobriety I heard a crusty old guy say, "Sometimes it just takes guts," and that got me through more than one crisis. A lucky few have the obsession to drink lifted immediately. I wish. Sober a few months, I spent a night alone at the Macdonald Hotel in Edmonton. As I passed the bar on the way to the dining room, the urge became so strong I ran up three flights of stairs and locked myself in the bathroom, as if the gleaming bottles behind the bar were outside trying to get in. I filled the tub and sat there crying like a baby and blubbering that advice over and over till the craving passed and I could trust myself to order from room service. I didn't want to be a person with no guts. I had started and never finished so many things in my life. I didn't want to fail at this, too, didn't want to lose the happy feeling bubbling up as one sober day followed another. It had been so long since I'd felt that. I couldn't remember the last time I'd laughed till I cried. And one of my nicknames as a kid was Happy.

You'll develop your own strategies. One of mine had to do with my right eyelid. Toward the end, after a night of heavy drinking, it would droop so that the eye was open only about the width of a dime and, try as I might, standing in front of the bathroom mirror, I could not open it any farther. (I later read that heavy drinking can paralyze a muscle like that.) So if I had to go where drinks were served—which was everywhere, it seemed—I'd look at myself in the mirror and say, "When you come home tonight and walk, not fall, up the stairs and into the bathroom, you will look in the mirror with both eyes open and say, 'You didn't take a drink tonight, you wonderful, brave person you.'" An E.B. White essay talks about someone glimpsing, in the jungle of fear (as he had so often glimpsed before), "the flashy tailfeathers of the bird Courage." I know exactly what he meant.

At some point a sneaky little thought will probably jump into your head and whisper seductively in your ear, *Maybe you're not an alcoholic.* I heard it at a meeting in a jail, with inmates telling their horrific stories and a chairman wise enough to look at us and smile. "If anyone out there is thinking maybe you're not an alcoholic," he said, "I can assure you that social drinkers don't sit around wondering if they're alcoholics." Damn! In my head I had already poured myself a drink as soon as I got home. And quite excited I was about it, too. Speaking of social drinkers, my alcoholic friend Clint says when he tries to pour his wife and his aunt a second drink, they tell him, "Oh, no thanks, I'm beginning to feel it." *No thanks, I'm beginning to feel it???*

You aren't comfortable without your old friend Booze to soften the edges and probably won't be for a while. I remember thinking the fun was over; you know, all that fun I've been telling you about. But you know what? Living without alcohol is a very interesting experience.

You start noticing things more. Jeez, when did all those big buildings go up downtown? Odd things will make you cry, like a hole in the stocking of a small Christmas angel. You'll be struck by beauty: red flowers against a yellow wall; the arch of your black cat's neck as he washes himself; blue jays in a snowy tree—were they always that exquisite shade of blue? Those words from "Amazing Grace" say it much better than I ever could: "I once was lost, but now am found, / Was blind but now I see." I don't believe there's a recovered alcoholic who isn't affected by that song. Believe me, you're going to feel so much more, you'll have moments of wanting not to feel so damn much.

But mostly you're going to love life again. The happiness of getting through the first barbecue with your old drinking friends sober. Surviving a wild kids' birthday party without sipping from a drink in the cupboard. Discovering you can go on a holiday and enjoy yourself while everyone else still drinks. Laughing the way you used to. Just feeling good.

Your world is about to get a whole lot bigger, Laura, and I'm excited for you. Just remember what you said last night: you want to stay sober more than you want to drink.

The rest will come.

HOW TO QUIT SMOKING IN FIFTY YEARS OR LESS

PETER GZOWSKI

As I WRITE, the odometer on my computer for the solitaire game called Klondike has just clicked over at 13,500 hands. My ten best scores have all been rung up since June of 2000, but I started long before that, getting faster, if not better, all the time. I'm so fast now I can open the file, knock off a couple of games while I'm still thinking of how to answer an email, and close it again before you'd notice. But let's say every game takes a minute. That's 13,500 minutes: 225 hours. Six thirty-five–hour weeks. Not counting research, I once wrote a book in not much more time than that.

Klondike is classic solitaire: red nine on black ten, black ten on red jack. The number of decisions you make is minuscule, and if you take a wrong turn you can have what golfers call a mulligan, press UNDO and go back. So what's the point? I have no idea. Yet without warning, I'll find myself stopping in mid-paragraph to . . . There, dammit, I've done it again. Opened the file while you weren't looking. 13,504. And if I hadn't stopped then, I might have played all morning. Many days it's as if I can't get going at the keyboard if I don't play a little Klondike first.

I'm the same with the *Globe and Mail* cryptic crossword. I'm convinced I need it to kick-start my mind. When *Morningside* went on the road in the years I was hosting it, I'd get someone to fax me the *Globe* puzzle as soon as it hit the streets in Toronto. Which would confuse my colleagues in, say, Inuvik, but keep me from twitching. At least I can understand the appeal of the cryptic—it's a contest between you and the usually anonymous puzzle-setter, and there's a pleasure in winning. There's even a kind of brother- (and sister-) hood of crypticians who nod to each other across the aisles of airplanes when they see a *Globe* opened at the appropriate page, although the quickest way to lose your membership is to dare to give someone an answer he hasn't asked you for.

And, oh, hell, I watch *Frasier*, too—every weeknight, on a channel that seems to have archived his every move since he left *Cheers*. His program comes on at 6:30 in Toronto, right after a CBC hybrid called *Canada Now*. There are worse routines of TV watching, I'm sure, and lots of less worthy expressions of U.S. popular culture than sitcoms. But I still feel out of control as I slouch deeper into my favourite chair, wave farewell to Ian Hanomansing, and tune in to the latest misadventures of a self-centred snob and his clearly unbalanced younger brother, whose nose bleeds when he fibs. If these guys are psychiatrists, no wonder we're all a little nuts. 13,506, 07, 08, 0 . . .

Klondike, cryptics, *Frasier.* Coffee (though I'll come back to that). Ritz crackers with peanut butter, going sockless until December, correcting other people's grammar, writing down phone numbers but not the names of their owners, saying "gonna," flicking mindlessly through the channels at three in the morning—all things I do but am convinced, rightly or wrongly, I could stop any time I set my mind to it. The difference between those habits, if habits they are, and what I think we mean by addictions is at least three-fold, the folds being:

1. With the possible exception of my compulsive channel hopping, I'm not hurting anyone else when I indulge in them;
2. If I were to stop playing Klondike or doing morning cryptics or baring my bony white ankles to the autumnal breezes, I would almost certainly not start shaking and retching from withdrawal; and
3. The price of continuing with these pastimes would not be death.

—

CONSIDERING WHAT smoking came to mean to me—there are almost no photographs of me after the age of seventeen in which I do not have a cigarette either in my hand or dangling from my lips, and no stories written about my times on radio or television without at least a mention of my lighting-one-after-the-other habit—not to mention what it means to me now, when I am pretty well confined to barracks with an oxygen tube up my nose and a four-wheeled buggy, like a baby's pram without the baby, that enables me to walk from one end of the apartment to the other . . . considering that, and all the other ways smoking and its effects have taken over my existence, it is perhaps surprising that I can't remember my first cigarette.

Of course, unless you count the time the apple-cheeked daughter of a farm family on the edge of town pinned me to the barnyard sod and brought a hitherto unknown—well, unknown in someone else's company—feeling to my loins, I can't remember the first time I had sex, either. And wherever it occurred, I'm sure my initiation to smoking was less pleasant than my barnyard romp. It still bemuses me, in fact, that something that became so hard to stop was, all those many years ago, so hard to start. I can't remember if cigarettes ever actually made me throw up—certainly my first cigars did, later on—but I can vividly recall the world spinning after a few puffs, my eyes running and my stomach heaving, as if I'd given myself the instant flu. Furthermore, cigarettes tasted awful.

So why did I start? Don't be silly. We all started. We had to. It was what you did, as much a part of approaching manhood as our cracking voices and the hair that was sprouting in all the predicted places. Girls? I'm sure they were experimenting with smoking, too, but in my memory the rites of cigarettes were as segregated as the skating rinks where we spent our winter afternoons, two rinks to a park: one, with boards, for the boys and the young men, and a second, with snowbanks, for the little kids, the sissies and the figure-skating girls.

If I smoked corn silk or any other boyhood imitations of tobacco, I don't remember doing it. I don't know where I would have learned. *Chums* or *The Boy's Own Annual*, which steered me through everything from the rules of cricket to the best way to make papier-mâché puppets (you model the head over a Vaseline-smeared light bulb) would have been no help, and Ernest Thompson Seton, my guide to all things natural, had other matters on his mind. So my smoking cronies and I found ways to come up with tailor-mades, though I didn't learn to call them that until much later. We filched them from our mothers' purses and our fathers' dressers or scrounged them from older siblings or, when flush with our allowances or snow-shovelling money, bought them ourselves, telling the shopkeeper, if he cared—and no one seemed to—that we were running an errand for someone else. Players, Export A, Buckingham, Turret, Sweet Caporal, Winchester, Sportsman (with its drawings of fishing flies on the yellow package) or, exotically, the menthol-flavoured Kools. We tried them all, discussing their various merits. We smoked furtively, cupping our hands around the glowing embers as we passed our elders on the streets, proud of our increasing ability to inhale without coughing.

—

IT'S CLEAR, I TRUST, that I am not yet talking about an addiction. A pastime, maybe. Something to do, always in and with company. We were social smokers, lighting up not because of how it made us feel, which was still more often queasy than high, but of how we wanted the rest of the world to see us—grown-up, cool (if that catchall adjective had begun to trickle down from the remote world of jazz), downtown. "I'm dying for a cigarette," we would whisper conspiratorially to each other at Friday evenings' Teen Canteens, when what we were really dying for was a break from the self-consciousness of dancing. But if cigarettes had disappeared from the face of the earth overnight, the extent of our withdrawal symptoms would have been a disappointed "Aw, shit, what'll we do now?"—not unattached, I'd say, to a certain sense of relief.

A lifetime later, when people who loved me or were worried about me or, in some cases, were paid a lot of money to figure out why I persisted in a habit that was so clearly shortening my days among them, would ask me why I didn't quit, I could sometimes do no better than "I smoke because I smoke." In the absence of a reason not to—a municipal bylaw, a coughing child, a disapproving hostess, the knowledge that an open flame might blow me and everyone in the room to kingdom come—it was simply a lot easier to light up than to forbear. Unless I consciously stopped myself from doing so, I smoked. Even when I was sucking back three large packages a day—seventy-five cigarettes, which is about as many as you can get through if you're still going to sleep a few hours—there were very few that I actually decided to smoke. The first one in the morning, sure, though that was more a reflex than an act of free will, my hand reaching across the alarm clock before my feet were ready to hit the floor, and the last one at night. A cigarette after each meal or task completed, and certain others through the day—to pick myself up, to relax, to sharpen my appetite or ease the pangs of hunger. But most of the time, I smoked without thinking, often not realizing I had lit a cigarette until I noticed it burning in the ashtray. Would I have gone into withdrawal if I'd stopped then? Absolutely. Even the first hour of a transcontinental flight would have me drumming my fingers and looking at my watch, and on the rare occasions I could be talked into going to a nonsmoking restaurant or accepting an invitation to a house with no ashtrays, I seldom made it to dessert without having to go for a walk. Over the years, I never really gave the storm clouds of abstinence time to gather. I just lit another cigarette.

—

MY MOTHER SMOKED Winchesters. She was the most glamorous woman not only in my life but in the whole of Galt, so far as I was concerned, if not the entire western world. She was a divorcée, the daughter of a well-to-do Toronto lawyer (or well-to-do until 1929, at least), alumna of a Toronto private girls' school, a Swiss lycée and a British university, still not quite thirty when she remarried into small-town Presbyterian Ontario, by day the children's librarian and by night a willowy star of both mixed-doubles badminton and such Galt Little Little Theatre productions as Noel Coward's *Blithe Spirit.*

My father had smoked Winchesters too, before he'd left for Depression-era vagrancy and, eventually, war. Their marriage lasted not much longer than a couple of flat fifties, barely time enough for me to pop onto the scene in 1934. Margaret, as the world called her, struggled for a while as a single mother in Toronto after divorcing my vagabond father and then—largely, I've always been convinced, so I'd have an untroubled home to grow up in—married Reg Brown of Galt, Ontario, who was the sales manager of a local textile mill and, because of a childhood ear injury, ineligible for war.

Galt, a prosperous city of some 18,000 on the Grand River (it has since been absorbed into the much larger Cambridge), was an idyllic place to be a kid. I was five when we moved there. We lived in an upper duplex overlooking Dickson Park, home of the Galt Terriers of the Intercounty Baseball League and site of both the annual fall fair and the skating rinks that were the centre of my childhood winters. It was an easy bicycle ride down Water Street to my mother's daytime headquarters on the second floor of the Carnegie library and to the hustle and bustle of a busy market town, with its principal intersection—Main and Water—marked by four imposing banks, one to a corner. But just as convenient in the other direction were the deciduous woods, murmuring streams and stone-fenced farmlands of pastoral Waterloo County.

As clear a memory as any I have of boyhood is the winter day of *verglas*, when a soft overnight rain was snap-frozen on top of a county-wide bed of snow. With the sun glittering off the land, the puck from our morning hockey game skittered over the boards. As we chased it, the blades of our skates skimmed across the frozen veneer. We took off, first out to the edge of the park, then hopping the fence, skates and all, out onto Blair Road and across the rolling farmscape, slaloming into the valleys, sidestepping up the hills, gliding across pastures and fallow fields, as free, for that one sparkling day, as the gulls that soared over the riverbanks. It was, as I say, the perfect place to be a boy.

"You smoke, don't you?" my mother said one day when I was fourteen, apropos, so far as I could tell, of nothing.

"Well, sort of. I . . ."

"Peter?"

"Yes. Yes, I do, actually."

I can see her still, clad in her slip, sitting at her dressing table's triptych of mirrors in the sunny bedroom she shared with my stepfather. We often talked there. I would perch on one of the twin beds as she finished her makeup for an evening out, tried on a piece of her family jewellery, or stained her long legs a silken brown, carefully painting a faux seam from her heel to the back of her knees. Later, I would come to realize how troubled she was in those times, how penned in she had come to feel in Galt and by her second marriage, but if there were signs of it in our early-evening chats, they were not discernible by my adolescent antennae. I loved my times alone with her, and she, I think, took pleasure in my company. She would tell me tales of her childhood summers on her father's hobby farm or of her schooling in Europe or, sometimes, if Reg were not around, of how kind my father's family had been to her after he had left his fledgling marriage—and his fledgling—to seek his fortune. On the rare occasions we actually talked about my father, she took pains not to criticize him. "You remind me of him," she would say from time to time, echoing observations I'd often heard from my Gzowski grandparents.

On the matter of my smoking, I think she was more amused than angry, maybe even secretly pleased that I had taken another step on the road to manhood and independence. "Look," she said, "if you're going to do it, you don't have to sneak around." She opened the pale-blue package with its red and gold lettering, pushed up the tip of a Winchester, and held it out toward me. "Here," she said, smiling, and reached for her Ronson lighter.

—

DOES ANYONE HONESTLY believe we didn't know smoking was bad for us? We may not have realized it would eventually kill us, or suspected it could rock us back on our heels the way I'm now rocked—I have what the health care system, bless its heart, calls COPD, for Chronic Obstructive Pulmonary Disease, but which everyone knows really means emphysema, just as acne really means boils and pimples. We probably hadn't heard of lung cancer or considered the devil's catalogue of other afflictions the world now understands are caused by smoking. But everyone knew that cigarettes did something different to your body than, say, asparagus. "That'll stunt your growth," people would say. Or "Sounds like a smoker's cough to me." Danger? If we'd even admitted there was any—a difficult concession to pry from a teenager about anything—it would only have added to the allure.

No, I'm afraid I can't pass the buck for my weakness quite as easily as do the people who've been launching class-action suits. Good luck to them, I guess. I have no sympathy for anyone who works for the merchants of death the tobacco companies have turned out to be, and if lawsuits help to put them out of business, then so much the better. But tobacco companies and their shills didn't start me on the path to the oxygen tent. I'd no more think of suing them than I'd think of suing Humphrey Bogart.

—

I LEFT GALT THE next year. I was screwing up in high school, a better pool shot than a Latin scholar, miserable at home. During the Christmas break of Grade 11, I went to Toronto to look up my father. With some reluctance, for he was working on a new relationship at the time, he took me in, then packed me off to Ridley College, his old boarding school in St. Catharines.

Smoking was a caning offence at Ridley, which was proud of its football teams. The penalty was ten painful whacks across the rump delivered by the headmaster. Legend had it, though no one made the roster during my time there, that the most exclusive society in the school was the "Armchair Club," whose entry requirements were ten times ten strokes of the cane. I didn't come close to qualifying. The only time I would ever feel the sting of the cane at Ridley was following an episode in which my entire Grade 12 class slipped out one night, climbed aboard a secretly chartered bus, and made our way across the river to the iniquitous United States. We were caught trying to sneak back into school, our heads spinning and our boasts of how drunk we were echoing in the midnight air. But there was a certain panache about defying the smoking law, and in due course I learned how to smear toothpaste onto my gums to mask the smell, how to dry loose tobacco on a dormitory radiator, and, most enterprising of all, how to steam up the communal shower in the basement of our residence so I could stand near the back wall, naked as a kewpie doll, and smoke a cupped cigarette down to its soggy dregs.

In the first summer after I'd been at Ridley, my mother died. She was thirty-nine. She was buried in Galt, and my father came to the funeral. He still smoked Winchesters, I noticed. I went back to school in the fall, and though I remember little of the next year, with the compulsory study sessions every evening my marks started to go up. In my graduating year, I made the first football team and stopped smoking for the season. But a broken hand suffered in practice ended my career. As soon as I could get back into that basement shower, draping a towel over the plaster cast that covered my wrist and hand, I lit up again. By the time I enrolled at university the next fall—on a couple of scholarships, thanks to Ridley's discipline—I was pretty well hooked.

IF YOU'RE GOING to quit, people would advise me, you should first try to cut out the things you associate with smoking. Well, sure, I would think, except in my case I'd have to cut out waking up in the morning, going to the bathroom, having coffee, answering the phone, driving my car, writing, talking on the radio, playing board games—or even golf—meeting strangers, watching television, having a drink, finishing sex (how else do you know when it's over, I used to joke, not knowing that the smoking itself would eventually look after that) or going to sleep at night.

Winchesters, brand of my youth, went off the market. I switched to Buckinghams, another unfiltered blend that was a perennial leader on the charts of tars and other poison ingredients. I stayed with them for a long time. That was a Buckingham people saw me light up on the final evening of my late-night TV career in the '70s ("What are they going to do, fire me?") and a Buckingham I stubbed out in an ashtray in the office of Avie Bennett, the former president of McClelland and Stewart. Avie, a militant antismoker, had practically ordered me to smoke in his office one day. When I finished, he said, "There, I have butts from the only three people I've ever let smoke in my office—you, Mordecai Richler and René Lévesque."

Once, in the early '80s, I was interviewing the artist A.J. Casson in a radio studio in Toronto. He saw my cigarettes on the table.

"Did you know I designed that package?" he asked.

"No," I said.

"During my commercial design period," he said. "A lot of us did that."

I still have that Buckingham package, open, signed and mounted in a red shadow box over the desk where I write—my only original Group of Seven.

You can't buy Buckinghams now. I switched to Rothmans when Buckinghams followed Winchesters out of business years ago.

You can't smoke in radio studios now either—or in movies, waiting rooms, limos, lobbies, university classrooms, barber shops, hockey rinks, offices, restaurants—even, for God's sake, in a lot of pool rooms and bars. I was in Yellowknife, the last of the frontier capitals, when they outlawed smoking in government buildings. On my last day there, I asked a couple of German tourists how they liked the town.

"Fine," they said, "except for the prostitution."

"Prostitution?" I said. "In *Yellowknife?*"

"Sure," they said. "All those women standing on the sidewalk, smoking and looking up and down the street for customers."

"They're government clerks," I said. "On a smoke break."

By the time smoking had fallen out of fashion—in what has been, surely, one of the revolutionary social changes of our day—nearly all of my friends had quit. One by one, they fell by the wayside, driven not only by the now unavoidable realization that it was going to kill them but by a variation of the peer pressure that had got so many of us started in the first place. If smoking had once been smart, it was now stupid. You didn't brag about it; you were, if anything, ashamed. And what with constantly trying to figure out where you could go and when, depending on whether you could smoke or not, it was becoming more trouble than it was worth. It was, not to put too fine a point on it, a pain in the ass.

Yet still I smoked. My teeth were yellow and my fingers brown. My clothes stank and so, I'm sure, did my breath. There were holes in my sweaters and scars on my furniture. My computer keyboard was regularly choked with ashes. My car looked and smelled as if there'd been an all-night poker game in the front seat. Once, sheltering a cigarette in my pocket (shades of Ridley), I set fire to a favourite windbreaker, and more than once, holding a phone to my ear, I caught the acrid smell of burning hair. In 1996, now in my sixties, I went into hospital for surgery to fix an abdominal aortic aneurysm.

About four days into my recovery, a night nurse, the one who used to prowl the halls on in-line skates, asked if I'd like to get out of bed and go downstairs with her for a cigarette, joining that sorry gaggle of people outside every hospital who lean on their IVS, bare bums exposed to the winds, as they suck on the toxin that put them there in the first place. "Are you *kidding?*" I snorted. But my first day home, with the physical craving presumably under control, I pawed through my cupboards until I found a half-full package of stale Rothmans and lit up in the living room.

Why? I still can't answer. If anyone asked, and they did, all the time, I'd say I hated my habit. It's hard to duck the fact that I probably hated myself for being such a slave to it. The reasons may well be buried in the childhood I've sketched so roughly here, but if they are, it will take a sharper brain than mine to ferret them. Whatever pleasure had once been associated with pulling the little red tab to remove the cellophane wrapping, taking out the layer of silver paper over half the package (we used to save that paper during the war so the RCAF could foil the enemy radar), pushing out the first cigarette, tapping it lightly on a table, lighting it, and then sucking that first, biting, all-engulfing, twitch-stopping drag of the day deep, deep into your lungs: whatever pleasure had once been there had long since gone. I smoked, as always, because I smoked.

AT 9:30 ON the morning of February 7, 2000, I pulled into the parking lot of a four-storey building in the suburbs of Toronto, rolled down the window of my ashtray on wheels, and flicked the butt of my last Rothmans into a snowbank.

After half a century of smoking, I had elected to incarcerate myself where I might find help. I'd signed on at a privately funded institution that had begun by working with alcoholics and, over the years, had grown into a treatment centre for people with addictions that varied from gambling to hard drugs to eating disorders. I'm preserving its anonymity because privacy is what the Slammer, as I came to call it, provided me, as it did all its patrons, and I feel I owe it that in return. As well, perhaps, as my life.

I'd sort of tried to quit before. Under the guidance of a wise and caring GP, into whose hands I'd been lucky enough to fall after my surgery, I experimented with Zyban, the patch, hypnosis, audiotapes, acupuncture, therapy—whatever was going. Everything worked and nothing worked. My guardian GP looked up the patch in the literature, saw how many people were having heart attacks caused by smoking while they were on it, and warned me never, ever to light up while I was attached; I ripped the patch off and had a cigarette. Hypnosis, for all my skepticism (or arrogance, if you want to be picky—of course *I* could never be hypnotized) actually took hold momentarily; I nodded off in the subject's chair while the doctor murmured soothing words and came awake to find my hand rising involuntarily at his command. But I lit up in the car on the way home and never went back. And so on. I foiled every attack. The truth was my heart wasn't in it, and the more I danced around, kidding myself and others, the better I understood the essential truth of smoking cessation: you can spend thousands on personal therapy and professional guidance, or you can stick a carrot in your ear and whistle "Four Strong Winds"—if you still have enough breath. The method makes no difference. If you've decided to quit, you will; if you haven't, you should get your affairs in order.

I was in pretty rough shape as I climbed out of my car that February morning. My drinking, another family trait, had been heavy enough for the last couple of years that it probably would have qualified me for the Slammer on its own. I was wobbly of stride, red of eye and shaky of hand. When I was introduced to the physician who would later turn out to be of particular help with my various demons, I shook his hand and, settling into the chair beside his desk, asked if he preferred to be called "Michael" or "Doctor."

"Steven will do," he said, "since that's my name."

I cannot say enough about the help—physiological as well as spiritual—I received in the Slammer, nor about the support of the people and systems I have leaned on since. I stayed inside my suburban minitower for most of a month, tranquilized through the worst of the physical withdrawal, a fresh strong patch glued daily to my flesh, making it through the nights with sleeping pills. I tried meditation and wished I were better at it, attended lectures on dependency, and went to AA meetings, where, though I resisted the air of evangelism, I found strength in facing my own weaknesses—yes, I was an addict, powerless without help. Some of the wisdom, I think, began to seep through. I made friends with a sprightly menagerie of other addicts in the Slammer, not only the predictable range of problem drinkers but also teenage druggies (some of whom, I'm sad to say, seemed to know more about the chemistry of artificial euphoria than the professionals who gave us our lectures), disarming gamblers and a bevy of extraordinarily attractive young women who would eat with us in the dining hall, a dietitian at their side, and then, if no one stayed with them, go upstairs and purge themselves to starvation.

I liked all my fellow passengers, although some of my affection may just have been the companionship of shared frailties. However stupid their behaviour, I came to think, drunks and hopheads are often clever people. A twenty-year-old heroin addict, a promising athlete who'd been the apple of her father's eye until she wrecked her knees and lost an American university scholarship, beat me at chess the first time she played me. A burly NCO from the Armed Forces, whom I initially had to coach on the finer points of Scrabble, scored two triple-triples on me in a single game.

My favourite fellow inmate was a jolly woman who had gambled away both her career and her house at the video terminals of the casinos. Hitting bottom, she'd reached such a state of despair that she staged an "armed robbery" on her local convenience store with a toy pistol, hoping that the cops would come and gun her down. But when I met her she was full of the strength she'd found in the Slammer, a dedicated Scrabble enthusiast, a passionate reader and the soul of kindness. She still faced a charge of armed robbery (it was later dismissed), but her real fear was that she'd wander one day into a provincial gambling den and be seduced not by the chance of winning her losses back—she was far too intelligent to think that was possible—but by the flashing lights and the unadulterated lure of excitement.

I had a special feeling, too, for the kids with eating disorders. Almost everyone else in the Slammer could be separated from their temptations—there were no cards in the common room, lest the gamblers succumb to pinochle for quarters, and anyone out on a day pass was liable to face a blood test on return—but everyone, including the young bulimics, had to face food every day. I would think of them after breakfast, as I watched my Scrabble partners and companions in group therapy step outside the swinging doors to smoke in the winter air, while I stayed inside.

Yet something worked. Gradually, and with a lot of help, I realized that I really did want to quit. By the time I was ready to retrieve my car from the parking lot (friends had arranged to have it taken away, vacuumed and returned ash-free), I felt like an ex-smoker. I'm still paying the price for my years of transgression. The emphysema—sorry, COPD—that now dominates my life didn't really strike until

I'd been out for a few months and was hit by a chest infection. I've had rehab for that, too, in a different kind of institution, and I work on getting better every day. It's a long haul. But a year and many thousands of games of Klondike after I tossed out that last cigarette butt, I haven't smoked again.

Oh, yes, I said I had a point to make about coffee. It's something else I learned in the Slammer. I'd been drinking coffee at least as long as I'd been smoking when I checked in. I *knew* I was addicted to caffeine, that I couldn't possibly start the day without a jolt, the stronger the better. When, as my recovery began, my hands finally stopped shaking enough for me to get a cup of coffee to my lips, all I could say was, "Thank God, now I feel human again." I kept that up every day till I got paroled. I was on my way out the door before someone told me it had been decaf all along.

MORE AND MORE

EVELYN LAU

When did it begin? The sensation of a depthless hole opening up inside me, a cavernous feeling of need. The surrendering to compulsion, which was like getting on a treadmill and not being able to get off. The craving for perfection, so that if I slipped and had one of something "bad," then the day had fallen into disarray, and I had to keep having another and another until the darkness fell.

It began in childhood, innocently. My normal child's greed for candy magnified until it became all-consuming, until the thought of the next candy crowded out every other thought in my mind—though there was little pleasure in eating it beyond the first sweet jolt on the tongue. After that moment it could have been soap or sawdust, but the urge to consume grew in me as steadily as an anxiety attack. The craving was compounded by secrecy, fuelled by being forbidden;

this was the most direct route I could see to escaping the control my mother exerted over me, to sabotaging her constant vigilance. Eating surreptitiously was a way of rebelling, of declaring my body my own. I chewed smuggled sweets in bed, tossing the wrappers into the darkness behind the nearby sofa until one day, to my mortification, my father pulled the furniture away from the wall to vacuum and found the dusty, crumpled evidence. I disowned responsibility the way only a child could, claiming I didn't know how the wrappers could have gotten there, it had nothing to do with me.

—

ONCE, VERY EARLY on, this desire for more must have had something to do with pleasure. Once I must have enjoyed a piece of cake or a scoop of ice cream and only wanted more of that enjoyment. But I can no longer remember such a time. I remember instead the growing panic, the desperate need that was a kind of clawing inside me. My quest for satiation blotted out everything in its path. When I was caught stealing a chocolate bar at a local drugstore, my mother screamed and hit at me wildly the moment I came home—was the food she cooked not good enough for me? Did I want people to think she was starving me? I had stolen two chocolate bars that day, but the store detective, emptying out my schoolbag, had found only one—the other had slipped between the pages of a textbook and lodged there. I hid the second bar in a drawer that afternoon, eager to get rid of it but unable to throw it away. The next day I shoved pieces of it into my mouth, fearful and ashamed, chewing miserably until it was gone. The chocolate was dark, it was bitter, it tasted like despair.

I hid sweets in my desk drawers, between the pages of books, even sometimes tucked inside my underwear when I came home from school, so that when my mother searched my pockets for contraband she would come up empty-handed. The food I ate became one of the few things my parents could not always supervise. Whenever they left me alone in the house I hurried to the orange kitchen as soon as I heard the door close behind them. Heart racing, palms sweaty, I ransacked the cupboards, consuming bits of food—a biscuit, a handful of nuts, a mouthful of whisky—that I hoped would not be missed. My mother had begun keeping meticulous track of the food in the house and forcing me every week onto the bathroom scale, which had the opposite effect of what she wanted. I was twelve, thirteen, humiliated by her mocking comments as she peered at the dial on the scale; though I was never more than ten pounds overweight, I must have seemed impossibly fleshy next to her own ninety-pound frame. When she asked me to undress, when she slapped my thighs or pinched my waist or criticized my large breasts, I detached in my mind the same way I would years later when strangers ran their hands over my body. I dreaded these intrusions, and my compulsive behaviour grew in direct proportion to her increasingly frantic efforts to monitor every aspect of my life.

Sometimes I would scurry down to the basement, where I would scoop up spoonfuls of sugar from the sacks in storage, gagging on the crystals lining my tongue. From my mother's purse I stole dimes and quarters that bought greasy paper bags of day-old cookies and doughnuts from the bakery on the way home from school. I still remember the taste of two dozen stale shortbread cookies consumed in a matter of blocks, the thick buttery dust of them in my throat, the nausea that pressed up inside me. I remember hiding behind a tree to finish the cookies before turning the corner onto the block where we lived, cramming them into my mouth; within moments I had reached a sugar and carbohydrate plateau where the clamour inside me dulled and my head felt thick, dazed. The storm of anxiety, of helpless rage, had passed for the time being. The frustration of never being good enough, of knowing I could never please my parents by winning a scholarship to medical school, of realizing that the life they wanted for me was not one I was capable of living. This happened day after day, bags of candies and pastries tearfully choked down along the corridor of streets between school and home. An hour later I would have to eat dinner, feeling so full I could hardly breathe, and that night in bed I would vow never to binge again; the next day I would wake up and be perfect at last.

But the next day I would wake in darkness, not perfect at all, and I knew I would do it again. I was driven by something larger than myself, some force I could hardly explain, let alone fight against. The tension that filled our household after my father lost his job, my mother's obsessive calibration of groceries and finances, my parents' expectations for my future . . . These things overpowered me and somehow manifested themselves in my need to keep eating until I was physically incapable of continuing.

It was as if I were trying to reach someplace that didn't exist, except in sleep or death. A perfect blankness, a white light. The search for this obliteration began with food, but later it wouldn't matter if it was food or alcohol or drugs or sleeping with men for money—the feeling was the same one I'd had as a child behind the shut door of my bedroom, gobbling up one candy, barely tasting it, so I could reach for the next, and the next. The urge was to keep going until the anxiety and rage stopped, until as a teenager I threw up or passed out or felt so blank that I no longer was myself.

ONE AFTERNOON WHEN I was sixteen or seventeen, years after I had run away from home, I sat sullenly in my psychiatrist's office with my parents. I wore a leather jacket and a miniskirt and was barely able to look at them across the room, my father's face lowered in pain and bewilderment, my mother twisting the strap of her purse between her thin fingers. My doctor was coaxing my father into telling me that he loved me.

"Chinese people don't talk about these things," my father tried to explain, haltingly. "It's not our tradition. But she knows. My wife—her mother—even when we couldn't afford any food, she would always have a cup of hot water waiting for her when she came home from school."

"She needs to hear you say it, Dad. Can you look at her and tell her?"

In a moment of what, even then, I knew was bravery worthy of a medal, my father lifted his face and looked straight at me. "Of course I love you," he said.

That was a moment I would remember from the session, though at the time I stared back at him hard-eyed. Also his mention of the hot water, how I winced at the pathos of that, and how my mother clutched my arm as my parents left the doctor's office and tried to persuade me to come home with them for dinner. Was it so simple as food equalling love? Was it their love I was after, in all the years of my life when I threw one thing after another into that bottomless well, and all of those things—food, drugs, alcohol, men—simply fell in and disappeared? What happened in the beginning that caused this? Something my mother did when I was an infant at her breast? Did she not come when I cried, did she hold me too tightly or turn her back when she should have stayed? Was there a chemical deficiency in my brain, a lack of serotonin, a predisposition toward these moods and impulses and compulsions? Was it a milder version of the mental illnesses that had stunted the lives of several of my mother's sisters, consigning them to a lifetime of antipsychotic medications and hospitals? Was it nature or nurture, creation or circumstance?

—

ONE SUBSTANCE REPLACED another, changing with the seasons. I gave up food for drugs, cigarettes for alcohol, moved fluidly back and forth, tried various combinations. As a teenager it was marijuana, LSD, tranquilizers, painkillers and cocaine. I binged on these drugs, finding a more complete oblivion through chemicals, a more extensive loss of self, of memory and pain. Candy is dandy, but liquor is quicker . . . and nothing is so quick as a few lines of white glitter, a syringe dripping with a morphine derivative. Even when the acid gave me bad trips, even when the world morphed into a greater nightmare than it already seemed, being high was still better than staying inside myself. I sought through drugs to be somebody else—anybody else.

At nineteen, when I stopped smoking three packs of cigarettes a day, I began my mornings instead with a drink in hand. That drink led to another and another, as the day devolved and the sun spiralled down in the sky. I no longer used street drugs, but started to mix alcohol with the prescription tranquilizers—Halcion, Ativan, Xanax—I obtained from various men, including the middle-aged married psychiatrist with whom I had a destructive yearlong affair. Twenty was a lost year, a calendar of blackout evenings, mornings where I could remember nothing of what I had said or done the night before, or how I had gotten home in the end. When I stopped taking pills, the bulimia that had come and gone in earlier times became one long unbroken stretch of binging and purging. I was throwing up seven or eight times a day and spending nearly as much on food as I had on drugs or alcohol.

Once, in my early twenties, I went out for lunch with two of my aunts. I was hungover from the night before. I could barely touch the greasy dim sum, and I lost my temper when one of them kept insisting that I eat. When we were ready to leave, I said I'd wait for them outside while they used the washroom. A few minutes later I changed my mind and went to use the bathroom myself; as soon as I opened the door I could hear them talking about me behind the closed doors of their stalls.

"I know why she's the way she is," one aunt declared, in Chinese. "It's not her fault. Her mother stayed in bed too long when she was pregnant, she didn't move around enough. I think it did something to Evelyn's brain, that's why she's like this. She can't help it, she's disturbed . . ."

I turned on my heel and slammed the door on my way out, enraged. How dare she assume there was something wrong with me? I refused to believe it myself. Yet that was how my whole family had dealt with my running away and becoming involved in drugs and prostitution—I was "mentally ill," which, in an odd way, absolved me of blame and responsibility. Once, to my psychiatrist's amusement, he received a phone call from this aunt, who insisted that I must be hearing voices; it was the only explanation for my behaviour. In her way, she believed I was pure, that none of it was my choice, that no one sane would choose such a life.

WAS IT A CHOICE? Many people believe addicts are weak, that their suffering stems from a lack of willpower, that an addiction or a dependency can be overcome by strength of character alone. Intellectually I lean toward this belief as well, but emotionally it is a different story. I think of how many people would like to have more than one cookie out of the bag they bring home from the supermarket. Some of them do have several cookies, savouring them, then place the rest of the bag in the cupboard. Others have a harder time doing that; they eat too many cookies, half the package perhaps, then feel repentant and disgusted with themselves. But imagine ratcheting that urge up further. Imagine that you are unable to sleep because of the cookies in your cupboard, that you can't work or read or leave the house knowing the uneaten cookies are there. That a feeling of anxiety begins to build in you, a desperation and a kind of anger, until you break down and cram the cookies into your mouth several at a time, devouring them until you throw up. If, after you throw up, there are still some cookies left in the bag, you have to keep eating them, even though by then you are sick of their taste and texture. If there are ten bags of cookies and no way that you can eat them all, you will have to bury the rest of them immediately at the bottom of the garbage pail—first crushing them and soaking them in water, say, to prevent your retrieving them later—in order to be rid of them.

Is this behaviour something that can be changed by force of will? The feelings behind that scenario: what are they? Are they symptoms of some other hunger, some emotional lack or faulty wiring in the brain? I don't know, but I have lived with those feelings, those uncontrollable impulses, all my life.

I don't like the word "addiction." It conjures up dismal pictures of sober or lapsed strangers sitting together talking about their dependencies week after week, year after year, mired in the language of abstinence and recovery. I find myself impatient with people who identify themselves so closely with their affliction. There is something in me that scorns the weak-chinned, bleary-eyed, sad-sack faces of recovering addicts whose lives and vocabulary have been overtaken by their illness. And yet the emotions they cycle through, the force that dictates their behaviour, must not be so different from mine.

Sometime toward my mid-twenties, the fog began to clear. Your body tires, your life changes, you climb out of the whirlpool and onto dry land. Certainly there were still days when I ate or drank to the point of vomiting, there were unhealthy relationships to become obsessed with, but I didn't lose myself in the same way any more. With adulthood came the knowledge that emotions and experiences that seemed decimating at the time would pass, and sooner rather than later. I was no longer always facing the end of the world. I became like everyone around me, with a mortgage and RRSPS and responsibilities, and if there were nights when I went out and drank too many martinis or glasses of wine, then stayed up all night throwing up in the bathroom—well, who didn't?

—

NOW I'M ALMOST thirty, the once unimaginable age. "Time to give up childish things," my psychiatrist chides. Once in a while I still binge and purge, but one lapse no longer triggers a six-month cycle as it used to. I often eat too much to quell some anxiety or emptiness, but now I can usually stop it from escalating into the sort of frenzy that leads to forced vomiting. Sometimes I drink vast quantities of alcohol and lose myself, but this is no different from the behaviour of many people I know. It's never a problem for me to have only one glass of wine at dinner, or to keep alcohol around the apartment without consuming it, or to go for days without a drink. Illegal drugs haven't interested me for a decade, and pills—well, there are vials of tranquilizers in my drawer that have lain there untouched for eight years. But a little part of me is still glad when I get a headache. Even the small amount of codeine in several Tylenol 1's makes me feel more confident and slightly elevated. So, after all these years of almost never taking a sleeping pill or a painkiller, I must still be cautious. The old desire for oblivion is not gone, only lying dormant, as are the temptation to slip into sleep rather than live through a difficult emotion and the longing to give in. And yet I know that if I give in, the next day will be harder as a result. That in the morning the previous day's anxiety, temporarily muffled by pills, will be back—tripled, quadrupled. That my hands will shake, my nerves will be frayed, and I will be less armoured than before.

The compulsions, the feelings of need and lack, are still there. They are always there. At one time, it was worth any price to get away from them—to feel bright and confident, to find the clearing in the forest where the sun streamed down and I was complete. I think now that these urges will stay with me for the rest of my life. The feelings will ebb and flow; maybe one day things will be a lot easier, and maybe they won't. At least I no longer wake up every morning expecting to be perfect, then destroying myself if I am not. Though I would never have believed it as a teenager, you do move beyond things, outgrow the person you were. Sometimes, just by staying alive, you find you have become someone who can live in the world after all.

BREATHING UNDER ICE

LORNA CROZIER

IT'S DARK IN THE back yard. Around eleven o'clock. Flashlight in hand, clad in my red flannelette nightgown, I search through the thick ivy around the trellis near the door, then in the woodpile and in the tin shed where we keep the lawn mower, garden tools and wheelbarrow. I've already gone through the shelves in the back of the bedroom closet, the dresser drawers, the filing cabinets, the laundry basket, the high kitchen cupboard that I can't reach without a stool. Outside, my bare feet getting cold, I move faster from place to place, afraid Patrick will rise from bed where he's been the past hour, turn on the porch light, and ask what I am doing. I pull the lever and flip the driver's seat of his truck forward, and there it is—the vodka bottle gleaming in the flashlight's narrow beam.

I feel elated. Charged. Vindicated. All afternoon I had thought he was drinking. Though I smelled nothing on his breath, there was that look around his eyes, the sideways shift of attention that feels as if a thin film of water has slipped between us and slightly distorted the way we engage. It's never anything I can be sure of, nothing I can put my finger on. He could just be tired, he could be distracted, he could be in the middle of dreaming himself into a poem. "Have you been drinking?" I finally asked. "No," he replied. But now I have the evidence: the fact of a cold, almost empty twenty-sixer in my hand.

I want to throw it at the moon, I want to pour the colourless liquid over the driver's seat and drop a lighted match, I want to carry the bottle inside, shake Patrick by the shoulder, and shout "Look what I've found!" Instead I tuck the bottle back in its hiding place and sit on the step, my head in my hands, wondering how in the world, at fifty years old, I've ended up here.

—

THERE'S A PHOTOGRAPH of my dad and me the night of my Grade 12 graduation. I'm in my first long dress, a sleeveless, aqua peau-de-soie with small covered buttons spilling down the right side. For the first time in my life, I have a hairdo. Ginnie at the local shop has shaped my curls into a bundle of sausage rolls on top of my head. Later I'll groan every time I look at my hair in this photo. Now I think it's as sophisticated as anything I'd see in a *Movietone* magazine.

Dad is wearing his only suit. It's the same kind most prairie men of his background and generation save for weddings and funerals, ignoring the shifts in fashion or their body shape. His arm drapes across my shoulders and, as he turns from me to the camera, his sloppy grin looks as if it's about to slide off his face. Before Mom snaps the picture, he says, "You're my little girl."

In the photograph our feet don't show. Mine are in satin high heels dyed the same colour as my dress. He's wearing his good oxfords, as they were called. Mel Caswell's wife gave them to him when Mel died. They were both small men with small feet, but every time Dad wears the shoes he complains that they pinch. If you could see the oxfords in the photograph, you'd notice that the laces are undone. After the picture, Mom, in a snit, sits Dad on the couch, yanks the laces, and knots a bow. He leans on her as we walk to the door.

We're close to being late for the banquet in the school gym a few blocks away. We *have* to be on time; I'm the valedictorian and my family is supposed to sit with the principal at the head table, where I'll give my speech after everyone's consumed the ham, scalloped potatoes and jellied salads. Over coffee and apple pie, my fellow grads and their parents will listen to my optimistic, conservative lines about the values our elders have taught us and how these will guide us through the years to come. There's no sense of teenaged angst, no disrespect or rebellion in my speech, no true words about what I've learned from my father. Though it's 1966, it's small-town Saskatchewan, and "the Sixties" are happening somewhere else.

The night before the graduation ceremonies, Mom and I knew there'd be trouble when Dad didn't come home. He didn't stay away overnight all that often, but when he did we knew he'd fallen into a poker game, probably at someone's farm, or a heavy drinking party that didn't know how to end. "It's always when something important is happening that he acts like this," my mom said. The last big public event in the family had been my brother's wedding two years before. The three of us had caught the night train from Swift Current to Winnipeg, where my brother was stationed in the Air Force, Dad with a bottle in his suit jacket, shouting and singing, keeping everyone awake until the porter threatened to throw him off. Shame was a large part of living with him, but that was the first time I willed myself to grow small, so small that no one could see me. Later I was startled when I caught the reflection of my face in the window of the train. I thought I had made myself disappear.

The afternoon of my graduation, my mom made me walk to the school to tell Mr. Whiteman, the teacher in charge, that my father wouldn't be at the banquet. He'd been called out of town for work, I was to say. The story was implausible because my father's job was in the oil fields, just a few miles away. I prayed that Mr. Whiteman didn't know what Dad did for a living, and I squirmed at the thought of lying to him. He was my English teacher, I'd just gotten 97 per cent on my Easter exam, and I wanted to keep his respect. Mr. Whiteman nodded his head and said nothing, but I saw something in his gaze that I'd never seen before. It wasn't disappointment or anger. Would I have known then to call it pity? Whatever it was, it made me mad, not at my parents or myself, but at him. The love I felt for my father was fierce and atavistic. It would have been easier if I could have simply hated him.

Now, a few hours later, I walk ahead of my parents to the school to relay the good news that my father is able to make it after all. The head table will need to be rearranged, my father's place card set beside mine. Trying to get to the gym before the other grads and their parents are seated, I walk as fast as I can, pounding my new thin heels so hard on the sidewalk that the rubber tip breaks off my right shoe. Mr. Whiteman is standing by the stage I helped decorate the day before with crepe paper streamers, Kleenex roses and balloons. When I move between the long tables across the floor toward him, one shoe makes a clicking noise; the other lands without a sound. I wish anything would happen but what's about to. I wish I were any other place on earth.

—

IN HIS BOOK *The Marriage of Cadmus and Harmony*, the Italian novelist Roberto Calasso distinguishes between two kinds of people: weavers and Dionysians. He explains that Dionysus "is not a useful god who helps weave or knot things together, but a god who loosens and unties. The weavers are his enemies. Yet there comes a moment when the weavers will abandon their looms to dash off after him into the mountains.

Dionysus is the river we hear flowing by in the distance, an incessant booming from far away." I was in my mid-twenties when I first heard that distant sound.

After high-school graduation, I went on to the University of Saskatchewan, in Saskatoon. In the middle of a four-year degree, I got married. My husband and I taught in a village in the north of the province for two years, then ended up back in my hometown, where I became an English teacher and guidance counsellor and he taught science. I was hard-working and responsible. My husband, a nondrinker, was as different from my father as he could possibly be. We lived on an acreage five miles south of town; we visited his parents in Regina every long weekend; we canoed, hiked, jogged, and went camping every summer with our dog. Life seemed conventional, predictable and safe. Then I discovered poetry.

At a summer school of the arts, where I went to work on my first manuscript, I met a group of writers I felt instantly at home with, and my shadow life began. We wrote poems, we drank, we danced, and a few of us had affairs during those three weeks spent away from husbands and wives. Many of us went back year after year. At the end of the session each summer, I'd return to my sober weaver's existence, threading together my marriage, my job, my in-laws. I began to think of starting a family, but I could hear that Dionysian river thrumming in my blood. I didn't know then it would soon drown out every other sound.

One day, Roberto Calasso says, the river "rises and floods everything, as if the normal above-water state of things, the sober delimitation of our existence, were but a brief parenthesis overwhelmed in an instant." I met Patrick, and the banks flooded. With barely a second thought, I pushed off from the shores of my previous life, left my husband and career for a stormy journey of lovemaking, fights, revelries and poems. We thirsted for intensity; we savoured crises. And right from the start, our passion for poetry and for each other included drinking. We had what fancier people would have called a cocktail late in the afternoon, wine over dinner, and sometimes a brandy nightcap before we went to bed. On the weekends we got sloshed and partied with friends. For our first ten years, the drinking didn't get out of hand. At least, neither of us saw it that way.

MY MOTHER HAS always been a weaver or, more accurately, a knitter. She likes to plant her two feet firmly on familiar ground, and she finds the taste of liquor in any form revolting. All the years when Dad stumbled home "drunker than a skunk," as she would say, she never touched a drop. The first Christmas after my father died, Patrick and I splurged on a bottle of Dom Pérignon. We poured glasses for her, my brother, his wife and ourselves, then proposed a toast. Before we could click our glasses, Mom took a sip, ducked into the kitchen, then reappeared beside us. When she raised her champagne again, we noticed it was dark. "It's too sour," she said. "I added some Coke."

Besides the few bottles of beer my father kept in the garage or in the basement cold room where the garden potatoes were stored for the winter, there wasn't any booze in our house. Dad did his drinking at the Legion, though he hadn't been a soldier in any war; at the Eagles' Lounge, which was open Sunday afternoons; and at the three hotel bars on Central Avenue: the Healy, the Imperial and the York. He'd get home from work, wash his face and hands, change into a shirt and tie, and leave for a few drinks before the bars closed between five and seven. He'd return to the house to eat the supper my mother had kept warm on the back of the stove, then head out again until last call. I remember how upset she was when the provincial liquor regulations changed and the bars stopped closing over the supper hour. Home from university for the holidays, I argued for human liberty, freedom of choice. "You don't understand," she said. "Now he won't even take the time to eat."

It wasn't that she was particularly concerned about his health. But without a good supper after working all day in the oil patch, where would he find the strength to get up at 6 A.M. and spend another eight hours at heavy labour? Food in his stomach would keep his blood-alcohol level down, too. Twice in three years he'd lost his driver's licence, a penalty that meant one of his fellow workers had to pick him up in the morning and drop him off at the end of their shift.

Both times the judge had allowed him dispensation to drive a backhoe in the oil fields. Otherwise he would have lost his job.

My father didn't lie about his drinking. What would have been the point? But never did I hear either of them use the word *alcoholic*. He drank, but he claimed he could hold his liquor. That ability was part of being a man, as was his right to spend his paycheque on anything he wanted. As was his prowess at arm-wrestling, shuffleboard and pool. The windowsills in our living room shone with trophies he'd brought home from the bars. They competed for space with the curling trophies he and Mom had won as skips of their own teams, though that game's prizes were often more practical—matching table lamps, a big wine-coloured ottoman made out of Naugahyde, a set of cutlery, a side of beef.

For Mom, his excess wasn't a disease; it stemmed from selfishness and a lack of affection for us. "He cares more about the Legion," she'd say. "He'd rather be with a bunch of drunks than his family." If he wasn't an alcoholic, if he could stop whenever he wanted to, the deficiencies were in us, not him. I wasn't good enough or pretty enough or smart enough to keep him home. Nor was she. He seemed to be having a good time, at least until he had to face her anger every morning before he left for work. She and I were the ones full of shame and anxiety and despair. We were the ones sitting at home each night, dreading his arrival, hoping we'd be in bed and could pretend to be asleep when he stumbled in the door.

—

PATRICK CALLED HIMSELF an alcoholic long before I was ready to hear it. I thought he was exaggerating. When I began to accept that he might be right, I admired his honesty, though the word *alcoholic*, like *cancer*, scared me. He needed to cut back, but what would it mean if he stopped altogether? Would I have to stop too? I didn't want to. After all, in our days of drinking, we'd had glorious times together. We'd written books; we'd received grants, awards and teaching jobs; and we'd been able to keep the vitality in our long relationship. We'd also done weavers' things: spent blissful days in the garden, renovated three old houses as we moved from place to place, built ponds, rescued and fallen in love with cats, and made extravagant dinners for our friends. Our lives were filled with shared passions, but also with moments of comfortable and deep companionship. At the same time, I'd recently found myself sinking into small pockets of despair.

Years before, I'd made some changes in my own drinking. I'd woken on a Sunday morning to one too many hangovers, one too many foggy memories of sloppy, embarrassing behaviour, Patrick's or mine. I began to question the equation we'd constructed when we first got together: one wild drinker + another = poetry and passion. I continued to delight in a glass or two of cool Chardonnay on my lips, but I'd cut back and, to my relief, the poetry and the passion had survived. There were still nights when I drank too much, but unlike Patrick, I could stop before the bottle was empty.

It's odd how living with obsessive drinking can feel fine one day and impossible the next. You wake up one morning and overnight someone has built a wall between you and that other life. Shouts and snatches of songs and conversations drift over the top, but though you long to join in, the gate that has always let you through remains firmly shut. I began to count how many glasses Patrick emptied compared to mine, how many times he dominated the conversation at a dinner party, how many evenings I had to drive us home. My tallies made me miserable.

Although Patrick had named his problem, he wasn't ready to do anything about it. I started to go to Al Anon, crying my way through the first meeting as if the years of sadness over my father's drinking, and now Patrick's, had funnelled into one narrow hour in a room full of strangers. At first I hoped my example would make Patrick see the light. How could he not at least control his drinking when he saw me heading out with such determination every Wednesday evening, a small book of daily meditations called *Courage to Change* in my hand? Didn't he love me enough to make me happy?

It didn't take many meetings for me to realize that he wasn't the only one with a problem. The eight or so people who sat around the table told stories similar to mine about searching for hidden bottles, about springing a son or daughter from jail, about lying to bosses and friends to cover up a spouse's misdemeanours, about doing everything imaginable to get the drinking to stop. Those who'd been going to meetings for a long time laughed uproariously at *their* bad behaviour. They laughed at how desperate and needy *they* had been. They even cracked jokes about living with booze: "How do you know when an alcoholic's lying?" "When he moves his lips."

A year after my first meeting, Patrick went to AA with a friend who'd been dry for eight months. When he came home, he declared his drinking days were over. We agreed there'd be no booze in the house except a bottle of wine, so I could have my usual glass before dinner. That didn't bother him. It was the high-octane stuff he craved, he said. Although I'd lose my favourite drinking partner, my own habits wouldn't have to change that much; everything was going to be okay. I was jubilant, but then the lying began. Patrick hid bottles around the house where he thought I wouldn't see them, drank when I was at work, and switched to vodka because it didn't smell as strong on his breath as Scotch or brandy. "Are you okay?" I'd ask. "Yes," he'd say. "Just tired."

Living with lies is crazy-making. Your perceptions tell you one thing; the person you love most in the world tells you another. Are you insane? Have you turned into a paranoid fishwife? How pathetic are you? Metaphorically, sometimes literally, you get down on your knees. You say things like "Please, tell me the truth, I beg you" and "Tell me anything, I won't be angry, just don't lie." It's bad for both of you, it's bad for the relationship, it's an erosion of trust, you tell him. How would he feel if the shoe were on the other foot, you ask, if the bottle were in the other hand? He doesn't pause, doesn't blink. He looks you straight in the eye and says, "I'm not drinking." You want to believe him, but when he's behind the wheel he swings from the yellow line to the shoulder, he asks you the same question three times, he doesn't remember the name of the movie you're going to. "Have you been drinking?" Of course he has. The real question is why in the world it is so important for me to get him to admit it.

—

MY MOTHER ALWAYS said "There's no better man than your father when he's sober." That comment made me furious as a kid. When was he sober? Why did she put up with it? I'm glad I had the sense not to push her for an answer. Limited by my judgemental child's eye, I had no idea of the private moments my parents shared. The afternoon she and my brother and I scattered Dad's ashes over the alkali lake on the farm where she grew up, she said "You made my life better" as the last of him drifted across the water. *Better?* Nothing could have shocked me more.

When I was fourteen, my mother got a job selling tickets at the Junior A Bronco hockey games. The rink was on the outskirts of town, a couple of miles from our house. She didn't have a driver's licence and couldn't rely on my dad to show up sober or on time, so she walked all winter through the dark and cold to the evening games. She did this for more than twenty years, until she was well into her seventies. Sometimes she'd get a ride home with a fellow worker; if not, she'd make the trek back again. I can still see her small bundled figure trudging through the snow, the icy wind whipping around her. When I call up the memory, it's as if I'm watching her from high above and she's the only moving thing in all that white.

She and I set off on several similar walks together when I was little. Once, after we'd waited for an hour for Dad to pick us up from the Eagles' Christmas party, a brown bag of hard, striped candy clutched in my hand, we headed out down the dark and snowy streets alone. Mom had refused offers of other rides. The temperature had fallen to thirty below, and she couldn't believe he wouldn't come. Halfway home, because I was shivering, she undid the big buttons on her old muskrat coat and pulled me inside, the back of my head pressing into her belly, the satin lining slipping across my forehead and nose. What strange tracks we must have printed in the snow as I blindly shuffled my feet between hers. It was an intimacy I revelled in, a return to the warmth, smell and darkness of my mother's body. Can I see it now as a gift my father gave me? Or am I struggling too hard to find forgiveness?

Sunday afternoons my father spent drinking in the Eagles' Lounge. When it closed, he came home with a Fat Emma or Pie Face chocolate bar for Mom and me, and after supper we'd eat them watching *The Ed Sullivan Show* on our first television set, a big wooden Fleetwood in the centre of the living room. A scrawny eight-year-old, I'd sit by Dad on the couch, as close as I could get, to play what he called "wrestling" and

I secretly called "the hand-hurting game." I'd bend back his thumbs until he cried uncle. I'd push the flesh of his fingertips over his closely bitten nails. This would go on for the whole hour, me trying to hurt my father. I delighted in our physical closeness, and he seemed to like my needy aggression, telling me how strong I was and pretending to be in pain. At the time I thought his cries of injury were real. I was always the one who initiated the game, and he patiently let me maul his fingers until I decided to stop.

Only now, more than forty years later, have I figured out what this all-consuming game meant to me. I loved my father's hands. Big-knuckled, strong from manual labour, they were often scraped and oil-stained. Harming them became my way of touching him and of having him touch me. It was our only body contact. I hurt him into loving me.

I don't damage Patrick physically, for pretend or for real. But I wound him in other ways. I know he suffers when he sees how wrecked his drinking makes me. Am I really *that* injured? Or do I play a martyr role, wet-eyed and helpless, to see his pain? How much of my adult life is darkened by my father's long shadow? When does the woman I've become fall away and that kid, with all her fear, hurt and anger festering just beneath the surface, take my place?

—

PATRICK IS A PERSON I can depend upon. When he says he'll be home at a certain time or promises to meet me with the car, he always shows up. Unlike my mother, I've never been that lone figure cutting through the cold while a man who has forgotten me racks the pool balls and knocks back another beer. But in my head, over and over, I've walked my mother's walk. Alcoholism—whether you're the drinker, the child, the husband or the wife—places you in a winter landscape. It takes you far beyond the warmly lit windows where other families gather around a table laden with their evening meal. It numbs you, it orphans you, it widows.

Alistair MacLeod's novel *No Great Mischief* opens with a family's disappearance beneath Atlantic ice. The narrator describes a small space between the water and the ice where you can open your mouth and breathe. As I read, I can't stop myself from seeing it as the place that drinking takes you. It's as if the Dionysian waters, without any warning, have frozen over. There are days when my own breathing space feels that constricted, that small. When I try to disappear in the train, when I lie to my favourite teacher, when I look for bottles in the back yard in the middle of the night, I'm there. And when I ask for the hundredth time "Have you been drinking?" my legs, treading water as hard as they can, barely keep my mouth above the surface.

When you're trapped between those two worlds, MacLeod's narrator says, taking your last sips of air before your body succumbs to the cold, you must look for a change in the light along the underbelly of the ice to see where you fell through. Then, while there's time—and there are only minutes—you must kick to the hole and hoist yourself up. That's what you have to do in spite of the draw of the long darkness below. I need to find the broken spot where Patrick and I went under. I hope we can get there together. Spreading our weight evenly across the ice, we will pull ourselves, hand by hand, word by word, over the wide expanse of cold and onto the rocky shore.

The excerpt from The Marriage of Cadmus and Harmony *by Roberto Calasso is translated by Tim Parks and quoted by him in "Adultery," an essay in his book* Adultery and Other Diversions *(New York: Arcade Publishing, 1998).*

THE EDGE OF DOOM

SUSAN CHEEVER

It begins innocently with a glance, with the meeting of hungry eyes, with a touch on the arm in conversation, or a hand at the back as you walk through a doorway. Perhaps it's a voice on the phone, mellow and somehow compelling, or a smell just below the level of consciousness, the slight scent of soap and flowers or tweed as you stand a little closer. The mind slumbers; the senses awake.

Then there is a conversation, or another meeting. Your life becomes dreamy with desire. When did it happen? When did the thoughts about this man or woman take over your interior life? When did everything else fade to black and white, while time together took on an almost painful, ecstatic vividness? Standing next to the object of your obsession, you seem to have turned gravity upside down; you have the sensation of falling and soaring at the same time. In a bar the bottles reflect a golden aura around your heads. In a restaurant the background music seems to have been chosen to describe your feelings.

Your love, for by now you are privately calling it love, thrives on obstacles. Secret meetings are so delicious that the rest of your life seems flat and boring. You feel possessed; nothing can stop the force of your feelings. When there is time for words in the sweaty aftermath of your fiery sex, you agree that this is something special, a once-in-a-lifetime gift that must be honoured. Anyone who stands in the way gets rationalized out of existence. She never understood me. He never paid attention to me. I've given a lot to my children already. I didn't really like this job. You don't think of what you are doing as unprotected sex; after all, you are not the kind of irresponsible person who would have unprotected sex. Instead you think you are engaging in nothing less than a physical manifestation of your spiritual oneness. You yearn to be even closer. This is the exhilaration of being drunk at the wheel of a car.

Your passion feels new, as if no one else has ever experienced it. That's what you think even though this sexual obsession is the oldest and best-known addiction in the world, consecrated in the French courts of love in the fourteenth century and in rock 'n' roll in the twentieth. It's also the most literary addiction. It has for centuries been the subject of great novels and escapades, from *The Great Gatsby* by F. Scott Fitzgerald to Flaubert's *Madame Bovary* and Leo Tolstoy's *Anna Karenina*, and from Shakespeare's sonnets to

Antony and Cleopatra, David and Bathsheba. Not to mention Adam's fateful bite.

Sexual addiction is less famous than alcoholism or drug addiction these days, but it is on the rise. Rehabilitation centres that treat sex addiction are seeing an increase in patients. Although in many ways this addiction is exactly like other addictions, it has been hidden in a culture that calls it love and describes it lovingly as a wonderful event. It feels like the weightlessness provided by the perfect martini or liquid Demerol or any other addictive substance, and the resulting relationship is filled with the cycle of yearning, requital and remorse that characterizes any addict's connection to his substance. "I think I'm falling in love with you," he says. He might as well be handing you a crack pipe. There is only one thing you want, and it shuts down all the other things you may have wanted in the past. That was then. This is now.

Recent research into brain science has shown that what we call love is an actual physical change triggered by the release of pleasure-inducing chemicals. Studies of prairie voles show that those remarkably happily mated creatures have brains teeming with these chemicals, while experiments with humans reveal that even a photograph of a loved one can release good things in the brain. "The complexity of the human brain . . . may mean that scientific understanding of human attachment may not proceed as quickly as some would hope, which will probably be a relief to the romantic poets among us," writes Steven Johnson, author of *Mind Wide Open: Your Brain and the Neuroscience of Everyday*

Life. Once you have experienced the warm-bath effect created by these chemicals, you will do almost anything to experience it again. When it stops happening with one partner, you will seek it with a new partner.

The first time I fell in love, my feelings followed the trajectory of any other addiction. This love had all the trappings of permanence. It had an engagement ring, and parental involvement, but it was as temporary as the courses we took together in the college where we were students. I didn't know W. very well, but my friends all wanted to go out with him. Therefore, I knew I adored him. For reasons of his own he seemed to feel the same way. We declared ourselves a couple, and I began to chase the delirious high of the moment when he had first called me and appeared at the door of the dormitory. I wanted to be with him all the time, although when I was with him we often bickered. What characterized this affair was my hunger for him, my willingness to drive all night or quit my job or let down my friends in order to be with him. That's what I remember. "Erotic love is the craving for complete fusion, for union with one other person. It is by its very nature exclusive and not universal; it is also perhaps the most deceptive form of love there is. It is confused with the explosive experience of falling in love, the sudden collapse of the barriers which existed until that moment between two strangers," wrote Erich Fromm in his classic book *The Art of Loving*.

When did it start? Like all teenaged girls, I was bombarded with Cinderella stories that suggested a man was my solution. I remember an afternoon party on a terrace and a talk with two famous men in the sunlight. As we chatted, a beautiful, willowy, tall woman named Blair, wearing a wide straw hat, wafted toward us. Her flowered dress draped against her in the summer breeze. When she floated away, both of the men hummed in admiration, an admiration I wanted for myself although I was just fourteen years old. I couldn't be tall and willowy. I couldn't be named Blair. I would never look good in a picture hat or be the kind of woman who made great men murmur with desire. But there was one thing about Blair that I could replicate. I could marry the man to whom she was married. Ten years later, not long after W. and I broke up, I proceeded to do just that.

Of course I didn't see it that way. I thought at the time that I had fallen in love with Blair's ex-husband the way the women in the books I read fell in love with their heroes, the way my mother had fallen in love with my father. It seemed a coincidence when, after my first marriage ended, I fell in love with and married two other men whose wives had every attribute I wanted for myself; they were models for *Vogue*, gourmet cooks, world-class homemakers who could transform a room with a few shawls. I was short and cute, with an educated wit that often crossed the line into inspired bitchiness. I couldn't cook, but I loved sex. Somehow, I thought that by seducing the men who were loved by these women I might become these women. Of course I had read Freud. I knew that, according to my therapist, all little girls want to take their fathers away from their mothers. I also knew that since I had some success in taking my father away from my mother—I often went places with him because she was too bored or too angry to go—taking a man away from his wife was an old, deeply embedded pattern for me. When I fell in love, though, none of that mattered.

It wasn't just married men. Somehow the love of an unattainable man, once obtained, made me feel whole. In his brilliant book *Love in the Western World*, Denis de Rougemont explains his theory that passionate love is always based on the obstacles to that love. Tristan and Isolde loved so keenly because of the sword that lay between them. Heloise and Abelard's love was forbidden and that gave it the power of a whirlwind they couldn't resist. At the French courts of love, the courtiers saw their ladies only from a distance—and this is still our ideal of love. It is not the love object that engenders these intense longings; it is the impossibility of union with the love object.

I don't like to think of myself as a sex addict. To me the words have a sleazy sound. They suggest body parts and clandestine couplings in the stalls of dirty bathrooms; they mean desperation and quick, ugly moments of release. Yet what about my longing to be a member of the famous Mile High Club, one of those who have had sex in airplane bathrooms? What about the awful recollection that two marriages foundered on my inability to be faithful to my vows, on a need for physical connection with another man that seemed to carry all before it? Yes, I was married, but when the man I had been "in love" with for years, the man everyone said was my "great love," came in from out of town, I found myself in bed with him almost before I knew what was happening. One minute I was calling his room from the hotel lobby to tell him I was there to join him for lunch, and the next minute we were moaning in bed together like lovers who had been separated for years.

Why did my friends always approve? "I'm in love!" I would announce, and they would rejoice. Everybody loves a lover, the song goes, and friends and family are no different. If the man I was in love with was married, no one seemed to notice. If he was a heroin addict, or deeply in debt, a fugitive from the law, or someone who hadn't made it through college, no one seemed to mind. Love was the important thing, everything else could be negotiated. Even my father signed on. During the Cuban Missile Crisis in 1962, when I called my family and expected to be summoned home so that we could all die together, my father told me about a dream he'd had the night before. "I dreamt you were walking down the street on the arm of a man you loved," he said as warplanes scrambled and President Kennedy tried to broker a few more tenuous hours of peace. "You were so happy!" What is love, then, if it is not that hot longing, that concern with every detail of someone else's life, that desire to possess? How can we love someone when our love is completely allowed and available, when there are no obstacles to overcome?

It wasn't until sometime during my third marriage that I began to change my definition of love. I was almost fifty, and the patterns of my behaviour became harder and harder to escape. I did the math. I began to see that infidelity, at least for me, led to disaster. It wasn't the damage to myself that concerned me most. My three marriages involved nine children—my son and daughter and seven stepchildren. By the time she was twelve, my daughter had lived through two divorces, more than any child should have to bear.

The burst of ecstasy I associated with first-time seduction and sex seemed to have an explosive power in my life far beyond its quick pleasures. I decided that this time I wouldn't cheat on my husband no matter what. That didn't keep him from cheating on me. In pain, I was aware that I had inflicted similar pain. Perhaps I just needed a taste of my own medicine. Perhaps I grew up a little. Perhaps the birth of my second child shifted my focus away from the pleasure of the moment and toward a bigger picture. I reached a bottom. The temptation to prove myself and punish my husband with another man was almost irresistible, yet I was able to resist. Somehow I knew that those feelings, those dizzying erotic swoons, were not love, and that in fact they might hurt the people I knew I did love—my children.

It sounds odd, but the closest thing to real adult love I have known has been with my ex-husbands. The two men who are the fathers of my children retain the qualities I loved in the first place, a fine, well-educated intelligence matched with a responsible heart in one case and a generous nature matched with a brilliant and eccentric mind in the other. Now that our lives are no longer entwined, I can appreciate them in a way that was impossible when we were together and when everything they did or didn't do seemed to have a huge impact on me. The quirks and foibles that drove me absolutely crazy when we were married have now become no more than that—someone's quirks and foibles. I don't care what my ex-husbands look like or even how they behave except in relation to our children. I remember with chagrin how their behaviour embarrassed me when we were together; now I can laugh about it. I can love them without needing to possess and control them.

Reflecting on my life, I see a pattern: one-third innocence, when I didn't know what I was doing; one-third addiction, when I was in the grip of unstoppable, misunderstood desire; and one-third recovery in which I have been able to stop choosing men according to some hard-wired fantasy criteria and start choosing them according to their actual character and behaviour. From here it seems as if my story will have a happy ending. I won't be half of one of those couples who grow old together, dandle their grandchildren, and know each other's habits so well that they seem like two parts of the same whole. But in spite of my great mistakes, I am blessed with two amazing children, and their love sustains me in a way that far surpasses any of those ecstatic lovers' moments I spent so many years chasing. At night, when they are asleep under my roof, the very air seems sweet with my feelings for them. As for men, once the intense focus of my existence, I have relaxed. I'm not sure what love between a man and a woman is, but I am fairly sure that I know what it is not.

"Love's not Time's fool, though rosy lips and cheeks within his bending sickle's compass come," Shakespeare wrote in his most powerful love sonnet. "Love . . . bears it out even to the edge of doom." You can say that again.

LOST IN A COSMIC SMOKE SHOW

ELIANNA LEV

EVERY DAY AT 4:20 PM—sometimes much earlier but rarely any later—I take out my weed kit and roll myself a joint.

I don't use pot for its sedative properties. Although I will smoke whatever is offered in a social setting, my first choice is sativa, the marijuana species, with strain names like "green crack" and "silver haze," that elicits a lively mental high. In my weed kit, which is a faux antique tin adorned with my mother's name, I also keep Zig-Zag rollies, a bobby pin for roaches and a lighter from the dollar store.

The tin was a gift from my mom, though I rarely think about that. After a decade of use, its insides are coated with dusty olive-green resin, and the tin is strewn with stems. I often wonder if it's a reflection of the inside of my brain.

Before lighting up, I settle into my swivel chair, put on a song and stretch my legs out onto the large green pot that holds the rubber tree next to my desk. The song I choose usually speaks to where I'm at emotionally: the Flying Burrito Brothers' "Cheating Kind of Love" if I'm dwelling on an illicit affair that should have ended years ago; Janet Jackson's "Love Will Never Do Without You" if I feel more optimistic. I let the song play for a few seconds, then spark up before the chorus.

For me, there's little satisfaction in vaping, edibles or capsules. It's the smoke that gets me off. Pot lets me bond with fire more than a campfire ever could. When I inhale, the smoke feels thick and robust, like the steady stream of a smokestack. It comes out straight but smudgy, with wavy edges like a chemtrail, or thin and elegant, twirling like a ribbon in a rhythmic gymnastics routine. I watch as these ghostly streamers expand and dissipate, along with the feelings I'd been absorbed in only moments earlier.

Sometimes when I breathe out, I channel the smoke through my nose, picturing a regal dragon. Or I do a variation on a French inhale; I let my lower jaw drop and jut forward slightly as I roll the see-through carbon around in my mouth, then trace my tongue along the roof to release it, while gently inhaling through my nose. I love that my body is capable of producing this beautiful malleable cloud and that my lungs are powerful enough to take it in. It feels like a skill acquired only by those who are fully committed.

I'm inarguably attached to the substance U.S. president Barack Obama described as a "bad habit and a vice." I often brood on this. My two-joint-a-day routine might impress certain Wiz Khalifa–obsessed teenage boys, but as a thirty-five-year-old writer who has spent the last ten years getting high, I often feel like it's time to grow up.

Because of that, I ask myself the same question every time I light up.

Do I really need to do this?

The answer is always the same: *What's the other option?*

And so, I get stoned. I am resigned to this habit.

—

AS A FREELANCE writer, I spend a lot of time alone. I've also been single for six years, and aside from a Chihuahua–blue heeler mix who is my ultimate spirit animal, I don't experience touch—romantic or otherwise—on a regular basis. The most consistent male attention I get is from someone who's married. My other dalliances are deep but short-lived.

The one thing I have going for me is my work, my writing. It's always been what I do to sustain myself, financially and emotionally. I write anything that pays, from soulless advertorials to pieces I have more emotional investment in. But I always reach a point in the day when I don't know what else needs to be done (there's always something) or what else I'm supposed to feel (there's always something). What should I be focussing on or fixing? After working on assignments in solitary for hours, I desperately need a shift.

With pot, I give in to my inner child. Everything feels attainable and possible after a joint. Things will open up, I know. My problems won't feel as pressing. Another side of me will appear, and I won't feel so alone. Time and space will expand and contract, and I'll ease into the shift like I'm slipping into a Jacuzzi.

It doesn't take long for the effects to set in. Like bubbles rising in a carbonated drink, my thoughts are pulled to another place completely. Whatever mood I've been struggling with that day swerves skywards. Blank spaces—paper, walls, horizons—become an infinite light show, a kaleidoscope of exploding atoms. Magic is being performed not in front of my eyes but through them. The whimsy in everything is suddenly unveiled.

After a few tokes, ideas rush to the front of my brain. I often cement myself to the computer and write. Nothing is fully formed; it's just seemingly brilliant inspiration. About 60 per cent of the time, these ideas go on to live full lives as magazine and web articles or investigative pieces. The rest are puzzling non sequiturs when I look at them later—total stoner thoughts.

Sometimes I burrow into the blank pages of my sketchbook and draw whatever is around me—my dog, the church across the street, the trees in my backyard. I draw without stopping, trying to copy what I see. If I have a new album I'm just getting into, I'll lie on my couch and listen to it intently. When it's something upbeat—Stevie Wonder, Danny Brown—pot prompts me to dance around my apartment, put on a show for my dog, who follows along with her cola-coloured eyes from the couch, barely raising her eyebrow markings.

After an hour or so, things start to blur. My vision gets slightly foggy, and my eyes feel like they're coated in a sticky film. I'm trapped in a cocoon of lost ambition. The urgent inspiration is gone, along with the clarity. My mood flat-lines. I am neither ecstatic nor grumpy, just a gravelly-voiced, droopy-eyed, emotionally resigned shell of myself.

—

I'M THIRTEEN WHEN I smoke pot for the first time, with a boyfriend, in a ravine near my parents' house. I don't feel the effects and think nothing much of it. A few weeks before starting high school, I try it again with Jen and Shosh, a pair of childhood friends from the Zionist Socialist camp I've been attending every year since I was eight. When Jen's dad is staying at his girlfriend's place, which is regularly, we use her house in Toronto's Annex as a spot to hang out.

After taking a few hoots on Jen's fenced-in back patio, I cough wildly and retreat indoors. I've developed asthma that summer, though it's not debilitating, and I mostly use the puffer to get attention from my friends and cute boys. I take a haul on my puffer now, and things immediately feel off. A strobe light seems to be flashing, and time is ungraspable. When I see Jen putting a chair on top of the table, I start to panic that we've all been poisoned. My friends, who have parents who smoke pot and therefore have more experience, reassure me in a soothing, authoritative tone that I'm fine.

Jen walks Shosh and me to the bus stop. We're on the way to Shosh's house, where I'm sleeping over. I grow more agitated as we wait. I stop an older couple strolling past us, telling them I've taken drugs and need to go to the hospital. Jen jumps in to reassure them we're fine. The couple walks away, giving us a dismissive look. I wonder if I should trust Jen; she could have been poisoned too. I keep brushing the crotch of my pants, fearful that I've peed myself. I'm paranoid that I'm dying or that I've permanently damaged my brain. *What if I feel this way forever?*

Shosh's parents aren't awake when we get home, and we sneak upstairs to her bedroom. Before I fall asleep next to her on the futon, I hear voices and dogs barking back and forth between my ears. The next morning I'm relieved but baffled. Recounting the experience later to another friend, I adopt a serious and cautionary tone. I have now lived through the harrowing experience of drugs.

Despite my freak-out, I'm not deterred from giving pot a few more tries. The first time I get high without being overcome by paranoia, I wind up at a pool hall with a group of girlfriends. A clique of older boys whose attention we desire is known to hang out there. I lean my torso across a jukebox, running my fingers up and down it, lost in a daydream, while "I Touch Myself" by the Divinyls plays. My friends laugh and mimic me. The hanging lights above the pool tables give the room a warm yellow glow, which envelops me in a carefree happiness. *I could get used to this*, I think, and join my friends in their fit of laughter.

Pot plays a peripheral role through the rest of my teen years. I wear a pot leaf pin on my lumber jacket to express my alliance with counterculture, rebellion and edginess, despite not actively living any of these things. I admire friends who can handle themselves when stoned. They seem cool to me, effortlessly badass. I never have the confidence to hold my own. I'm too wrapped up in my moods, which are dark and weighty.

For Grades 9 and 10, I attend a WASPY high school in North Toronto. My classmates are the sons and daughters of wealthy Liberal politicians and high-profile Canadian actors. It's hard to keep up with this crowd of teens, and I resent how easy they have it. I go deep into my head, unable to articulate why I always feel so bad. At the suggestion of my doctor, I see a series of psychiatrists, though they don't seem to understand, care or even listen. I catch one doodling a squirrel on her notepad before she suggests I go on Prozac. I don't.

In Grade 11, I transfer to a small alternative school where we sit in circles, call our teachers by their first names and grade ourselves based on what we feel we deserve. Despite my insecurity about my appearance—I have a severe case of eczema, which manifests around my lips, forehead and cheekbones in raw, oozing blotches—I am happier here among smart fringe kids who couldn't conform to the traditional structures of high school. Many of them drink or get stoned during the spare time we have between classes. My brain feels too fragile for me to partake, except occasionally.

At eighteen, I decide to get as far away from Toronto as I possibly can. I head to the city of Victoria, sight unseen. I don't even know it's on an island, only that my new school, the University of Victoria, has a reputable writing program and the West has milder winters. The first year is lonely and jarring. I've downsized from Canada's largest most multicultural city to a sleepy white-bread town with an abundance of Ye Ol' Confectionery Shoppes. Over time, though, I bond with my fellow writing students. We put on literary events and take turns reading our work. Despite the slow pace of my new town, I fall for its salty air and winter blossoms. And I feel part of something here for the first time: a network of like-minded folks who celebrate one another.

During my third year at school, I move in with a boyfriend named Jon, a Phish head with no real aspirations. We'd met in Toronto through family friends, and he moves across the country to be with me. I know he's a pothead, but I don't understand yet to what extent. My friends soon nickname him Chron, a play on "chronic," based on his unceasing consumption—upwards of eight joints a day. He is moody and volatile, and screams wildly at me when I find us a basement suite where he's not allowed to smoke inside.

After Jon and I break up, I'm so put off marijuana that I don't touch it for five years. The end of another, more serious relationship changes that. A lumpy futon in a windowless basement on Vancouver's east side is my refuge during this dissolution. One afternoon I discover my ex-boyfriend has met someone new while on tour with his band —a willowy stripper from Ibiza— and is arranging to live with her *in our old apartment*. My mind is a tornado powered by hostile thoughts that refuse to slow down. When one of my new roommates gifts me with a joint, I light up immediately. Within moments, my agonizing fades. Thoughts of my ex dissipate as quickly as the smoke I exhale.

I move into my own place, a bachelor pad on a busy corner in Vancouver's Mount Pleasant neighbourhood. At night, a streetlight shines directly into my bedroom, and a traffic light emits beeping noises every few minutes to help blind people cross safely. My neighbour, a high-energy party girl, screams, fucks and cries at all hours, and our walls do nothing to insulate the drama. As a result, my sleep is uneven.

I work in a newsroom where I'm trained in everything—print, broadcast, web, editing, chasing, reporting—and end up as the fill-in girl, covering early-morning shifts, weekend shifts, whatever needs to get done. Despite often wishing for a more creative writing career, I'm grateful for this job, which is considered prestigious in my field. I get along with my co-workers, whip-smart, hardworking journalists who are always keen to teach me something new. My days are full and fast-paced, and I always end them the same way: by smoking a bowl of weed. Firing up the pipe is my ritual, a celebration of my independence, the moment when clarity goes up in smoke and things get a lot more fun.

—

BY MY LATE twenties, my attachment to weed is undeniable. At twenty-nine, I experience severe depression after the meltdown of what I thought was an intense love affair but was really just a casual fling with an equally unstable fellow. After I experience several manic episodes when I stay up all night plotting ways to keep this man in my life, my doctor suggests I take a break from pot for thirty days.

I fly back to Toronto, where my parents keep an eye on me. After being laid off from the newsroom during the recession, I've jumped into freelancing. Employment insurance allows me the freedom to do such a thing. It has also allowed me the freedom to get stoned during banker's hours.

My mother and father are aware of my pot use, though they can't relate to my struggle. The days are long and daunting when pot isn't around. To distract myself, I go for contemplative walks in the ravine. Nothing is fulfilling without pot; nothing feels worthwhile. Still, I manage not to give in. My mania doesn't resurface, but life feels flat. I return to Vancouver when my thirty days are up, and I pick up where I left off when a guy in a band I interview offers me some weed. Soon after that, I go on antidepressants. I continue smoking daily, but I start to question why. For the first time, my keen alliance with pot makes me uneasy.

I attend an NA meeting with an old co-worker from the newsroom. We'd been laid off at the same time, and soon after he'd admitted to a crack addiction. The energy in the Salvation Army hall is heavy, full of men in patched jackets with stone-faced stares and stories to tell. My problems are trivial by comparison. I'm much too soft to be here. Some time later, I pop into a Marijuana Anonymous meeting at a synagogue.

Many in the group are also struggling with harder substances, though there are plenty of recovering potheads who fit the stoner cliché: there are even two jugglers in the group, though they are strangers to one another. The meeting is easier to sit through than NA, but I don't return, and I start smoking pot again the next day.

In my early thirties, I share the top level of a heritage house with a midwife. She is personable, studious and responsible, all essential qualities for a job that involves bringing life into the world. By contrast, I am disorderly and laissez-faire; I love the lack of structure that comes with being a freelance writer. Despite our differences, we form a friendship, leaving leftovers outside each other's doors, swapping clothing and exchanging keys.

She stores her pot—two joints rolled by her ex-boyfriend that she's saving for a special occasion—in a Tylenol bottle in her freezer. I dip into her stash when she's away for a week. I've never stolen anything before, and I'm mortified. Soon after, I buy some pot, roll a joint and shove it back in her pill bottle. That doesn't get rid of my guilt. I'm weighted down and feel unsettled when my neighbour comes back. I'm relieved when I'm offered a job in Toronto and move out a few months later, before she has a chance to realize what I've done.

—

POT BRINGS OUT my stingy and insincere side. I don't usually like to expose it, but when weed is involved, I ignore my disdain for this quality in myself. I prefer smoking other people's weed over mine. My Toronto friends are mostly fellow potheads. I know where they keep their stashes, and they tolerate it, even find it amusing, when I help myself. They know that if I'm in a room with pot, pot is my priority. The shame I feel at this is stifled by my obsession.

The dynamic among my stoner friends is generally unspoken. Sometimes we are candid about it (*My dealer's out of town, and I'm all out!*). Other times there's simply an underlying energy that leaves little doubt (*I know I just saw you yesterday, but I'm in your neighbourhood again!*). The desire to get high is usually what brings us together. That way, we all feel a little less alone in our yearnings. Most of us acknowledge this as typical addict behavior, but considering it's "only pot," we don't dwell on it.

When it comes to romance, stoned sex is the best kind of fun, and the non-smoking guys I date never make a fuss about my enthusiasm for Mary Jane.

Still, I feel unsettled by pot's power over me, the fact that I give in to it so easily. It's the devil I love, but I convince myself it needs, at the very least, some boundaries. My plans to quit, however, consistently fail.

The process is always the same. First, I power-smoke my way through my stash. Next, I delete my dealer's number from my phone. Then I sit with the openness of the day, the depths of emotion that can't be quelled. I try to breathe through these feelings, but I quickly get bored. I think about how much more exciting my life is when I have some pot around, how other sides of me reveal themselves as a series of paper cutout dolls, stretching out like an accordion. Finally, I text a friend who shares the same dealer and ask him for the contact details. I program the dealer's number into my phone again and send him a text.

I consult my beloved naturopath, who has successfully helped me reign in my eczema. He encourages me to read a best-selling book about quitting cigarettes, which I do. I'm soon repulsed by the concept of cigarettes, but giving up an occasional social habit only helps me revel more deeply in the dank smell and musky, burnt flavour of weed.

—

SOME OF MY friends, committed drinkers, have advised me over the years not to wrestle so hard with pot. *Don't make it into a big deal*, they tell me. Their advice comforts me. I'm an adult, and this is what I'm choosing to waste my clarity, my focus and my money on. Aside from filing stories on time, I have no real responsibilities: no child to support in day care, no mortgage to stress over, no boss to act normal around. Drinking has never appealed to me, and I'm relieved by this. Hangovers waste too much time.

The fact that pot is technically an illegal substance in Canada—with confusing caveats when it comes to medicinal use—doesn't deter me either. It doesn't help that being a stoner is touted as a pretty fun club to be a part of. Take any episode of *Broad City* or the photos of Rihanna seductively taking a haul off a spliff. The celebratory attitude of reefer culture comforts me. The ultimate deal-breaker is cosmic cool dad astronomer Carl Sagan, who left a legacy as a prolific stoner. You'd think exploring and popularizing the cosmos would be otherworldly enough without marijuana. Yet Sagan chose to use and advocate for pot.

In my mid-thirties, I took up meditation in an attempt to level my depression. I noticed a difference almost immediately—a softening, a distance or pause between my moods. Eventually, I went off my antidepressants. As I got deeper into my practice, I learned a visualization technique where I imagine warm liquid sunlight expanding from my heart and cascading over my body. Clear-headed, I find this image a challenge. But when I'm stoned, when I close my eyes and catch the sunlight at a certain angle, the light penetrates to the back of my head and encases me in a warm golden glow. It's like floating to a different realm, somewhere heavenly. I feel a kinship with Sagan then, a mystic moment in an enlightened dimension.

THESE DAYS, POT is an afterthought, as engrained in my daily routine as morning pages, meditation and brushing my teeth. The glaring void that should be filled by a life partner, a family, someone's daily presence, is instead filled with smoke.

I've given up on quitting, and most of the boundaries I set for pot in the past are gone. I used to not smoke the night before a major meeting. I'd never go to yoga stoned, and certainly not to the gym. That changed when my freelance career stabilized. Smoking has never interfered with my writing, though it can certainly affect my motivation. When work is slow, it's so much easier to watch TMZ Live after smoking a spliff than focus on pitching story ideas.

I still don't smoke when I travel outside the country, since a nightmare of mine is being denied entry to the U.S. I always meditate long before I light up, and I commit to sobriety when I participate in alternative healing: sensory deprivation tanks or the shamanic journeying circles I joined in the last year. It comforts me that it's possible to experience something powerful without being stoned.

I rely on my own supply now, as an adult should, and replenish the day after I've smoked my way through a bag. Last winter, I escaped the unforgiving cold in Toronto and did a cat-sit for six weeks in Vancouver. While I was there, I visited a marijuana dispensary. My assumption that I'd be dealing with someone in a lab coat disappeared as soon as I walked in. The place was blaring dubstep, and a petite Asian woman in a see-through tank top handed me a form to fill out as she photocopied my ID. I waited with giddy teenagers and sheepish men in splattered painting outfits to talk to a doctor. When it was my turn, I walked into a room with an iPad set up to display a man on Skype, his diploma clearly in the frame. I told him I have depression. He asked if I'm on meds. Two minutes later, I had a membership and a $10 bag.

After being a pothead for so long, the dank smoke hangs on my breath longer than it used to. My middle and pointer fingers reek of weed, and crumbs line all my purses. Sometimes the spot where my fingers meet my lips is stained with a brownish yellow resin. I care, but not enough.

What should concern me more is the shift in my memory. Pot is either erasing my ability to remember or making my brain super lazy. I forget stories I've told hours earlier to the same people. I go blank on my favourite band in middle school. I wrack my brain for the name of that restaurant I lived across from for three years, with its lovely neon-blue sign. It takes a lot of digging to remember many things. I generally chalk this up to aging, but I wonder sometimes how much better I would fare without all the smoke.

I get stoned before a fancy dinner in Toronto for media outlets and freelancers hosted by a tourism board. I'm seated next to an editor from a lifestyles magazine, and I tell her about my idea for a story on visualization. She is interested and gives me her card. The next day, when I start typing in her email address, her name spells itself out automatically. I do a search of my emails and pull up a conversation I'd had with her two years prior, after I sat next to her at another dinner put on by the same tourism board.

I contact her and try to make light of it, seeing as she hadn't appeared to recognize me either.

"Yes, I remembered meeting you," she writes back. "You were in a different place then, different energy."

Like certain manipulative married lovers I've kept around too long, I'm aware of the power marijuana has over me. In the past, I've managed distant, even disdainful relationships with marijuana, and I'm confident I can get to that point again. I just don't want to at this moment. Maybe something that sounds good on paper—a serious boyfriend who's intolerant of smoke, a lucrative job in a foreign country—will inspire me to want to change. Until that point arrives, all I can do is resign myself to my pattern: roll, spark, toke.

DRINKING

DAVID ADAMS
RICHARDS

When I was four my grandfather, who'd been drunk for days, bought my sister a horse—a bowled, wobbly draft he brought to the front of our bungalow. We were at the door watching as my mother went out to meet him. She was pregnant again, and an outsider among her in-laws; an outsider in our town of Newcastle, in which we as a family were also in a certain way outsiders.

Though we were willing to care for it—house it in the garage, feed it beets—my mother broke our hearts by telling him we couldn't accept it. This was quite an insult in front of the men he drank with, who had talked him into buying it. So he cursed her in front of those men.

We did not get the horse. Nor did we know we were part of a power play Grampie had concocted, silly little dupes for the grown-up world. My mother putting her foot down on the edge of our dry lot quashed the grandeur he had tried to obtain by spending my grandmother's money.

My grandfather came to our house at breakfast the next day to continue his tirade, and my father, with shaving cream still covering half his face, came out of the bathroom and told him to leave. There was shoving at the door, but my father, though uniformly a pacifist, was as strong as a bull. So my grandfather left, hat and suit askew, railing abuse at us all.

My father didn't drink, for he had seen what it had done to his stepfather—our Grampie. I could see my father shaking as he came inside, in anger and bewilderment. Bewilderment for his uncles, who were numbered among the town drunks. They were men of my blood.

When I was little, drink surrounded me as rivers did fish. It lay in the burdocks and pissed its pants, or came at me zigzagging up walkways, answering to the names of forgotten cousins and family members gone off to Boston years before. It acquired taste and wore suits and carried on its person, in 1956, golden folded pocket-watch chains, or carried hand purses, and fashionable gloves, down to our one good restaurant on some forgotten May afternoon to order sandwich slices and rye whisky. It listened to elevator music in the offices of the movie theatre that my family owned, and could recite psalms and talk about St. Augustine. It had a yearning for sophistication never quite achieved, and ached on rainy days in the back rooms of small houses. It blossomed at weddings, got sentimental at baptisms; it carried the weight of a sagged paunch, had a sad grin or light whimsical eyes at forty. It trotted out bad poetry at St. Patrick's Day concerts and railed against the English all over again. And again. And again.

So before I ever drank or sang an Irish rebel song or shouted out in joy and rebellion, drink was part of me. And not only was there drinking in our family: we employed drinkers as well, at our theatre. The ones I admired were dutiful-minded; there was something great about their affliction—drawn to our theatre and each other, they had the mark of genuine humanity. They watched Bogie thwack the bad guys, drive a boat blind in fog, grin through his whisky and cigarette smoke.

Back in the fifies, when these men were in their twenties, they ran projection machines and took tickets, chewed peppermints to mask the smell of wine, stood waiting for drives home at dark in freezing weather without hat or mitts, more like Bogie than they would ever know. Sooner or later they drifted off or moved away.

Drink surrounded me, coaxed me gently with its timeless serenade, told me that it would wait, bide its time, and be there whenever I turned to embrace it.

When I was eight years of age my family moved to a section of town called "the Rocks" that overlooked the crystal Miramichi River. It was a harsher and wilder part of town, with families not only blue-collar but desperately poor. Here, on May nights filled with the whiff of snow, prostitutes as young as sixteen would wait for strange foreign sailors, accepting in payment foreign utterances of devotion and a bottle of wine. I passed them lying down on cardboard boxes in the flare of fires as I walked up the small pathway with my little sister. We saw men sitting out on the banks to drink who had, like my great uncles, been shot up in the first war or gassed at Ypres. I knew them by name, and was conscious of a certain decayed splendour they had.

By twelve I began to hear my name called by those who mocked what they considered in error my father's money and my lame left side, lame because of a fall my mother had when she was seven months pregnant with me. Because of this I was always something of an outcast. I understood that I was different and I suppose I was alone.

All of this was diligent recruitment for the bottle. Yet as a boy I could never picture myself with a drink in my hand. The only thing my father ever requested of me, on one of our trips to Saint John, was for me not to drink. Still I knew it was near me. Sometimes it came into the house with the cold, off the breath of some playful uncle, and slapped me on the knee and laughed. Or it coursed through the veins of certain bleary-eyed men my father did business with in Saint John. (I accompanied him only so I could go to a restaurant and have an elevator ride.)

At first on occasion, and then on a more regular basis, I began to see drink in youngsters I knew. They drank in caves or shacks overlooking the river, their faces drenched white by their breath or the light from weak light bulbs. I knew that soon something would be required of me.

The first two people my age I saw drunk were the son of a judge and a boy that judge had put in jail. They offered me a beer. I shook my head no. They mocked me. I went home. Yet, thinking of the reputation it carried within my family, I promised myself I would never drink. I made that promise in October of 1964. I began to drink that December, at the time I began to read books. I was given a beer on Christmas Eve. Flushed with lights and joyous celebration, all seemed possible. I was also given a copy of *Oliver Twist* that same Christmas, and my love of books and writing was born.

By fifteen I was drinking now and again, a bottle of beer or a quart of wine. Sometimes I bought it myself, staring at the bottle as a foreigner. Often the beer tasted like potato peelings, or the wine was too sweet. We drank in groups on special occasions. After a time there was no need for special occasions—whenever we managed to find something to drink, well, that was special enough.

Looking back now, I see I drank with many kids whose families had histories of drink. We were establishing ourselves as the next generation. From the first I didn't drink naturally—but neither did any of my friends. We came from a hard-drinking river, though, and after a certain period we all drank heavily, continuing until we quit or were killed or found ourselves chronic alcoholics.

I was discernibly different from most of my friends in one way. I literally *loved* to drink alone. If I was still drinking, I still would.

The town library had three floors, and on the top floor was a locked room. It was the French room, with French books, and a friend of mine had obtained a key. No one else ventured up there, and with the door locked it made a comfortable place to while away the afternoons when I was thought to be in school. I had no use for school, but, as I mentioned, I loved books. And many of these French texts had side-by-side English translations. So I drank wine and read François Villon in the old nineteenth-century manse. When the librarian locked the front door and left for home, I would venture into the rooms downstairs and read until well after dark. I also started to write my own sketches there.

As my drinking and skipping school became more frequent, I became more of a problem. I rebelled in a violent, almost anarchistic way. I came to class late or snuck in a bottle with me. Since I was small compared to others, I would fight at the least provocation. Finally I was suspended, then expelled. I was told the only way I'd be allowed back in school would be if I saw a psychiatrist and took the strap. I was in a funny position, forced to see a psychiatrist and take the strap in order to be allowed access to someplace I never wanted to be.

However, I did graduate and was accepted by St. Thomas University. Here I drank more, and partied harder. It was here that a friend took me aside and cautioned me one afternoon. If I was invited to his parents' house he wanted me sober. It was the first time anyone had ever said anything to me about my drinking, and it provoked me. I did not go to his house or visit him again.

During these years a number of friends and acquaintances I had grown up with were killed. Most of them died, in one way or another, because of drink. I wanted to write about all of this, and I started a novel.

But my writing seemed very much like everything else in my life. No one thought me much good. So I quit university and went to Europe. There I drank every day. I got drunk only once, but I came back home with an appreciation for the morning drink.

At twenty-one I got married to the girl who had stood beside me during my high-school visits to the psychiatrist. We lived at first in a room in Fredericton, with a hot plate and a single cot. The bathroom was two flights up. We got our own little apartment on King Street some months later, and it was there I wrote what would become my first published novel, *The Coming of Winter.* After that was done, we moved to another apartment, on Saint John Street, where I started my second novel, *Blood Ties.*

I was twenty-three, twenty-four years old. I was drinking almost every day and taking downers (which I thought were a great complement to a drink, and had gotten from the second psychiatrist I was asked to see). By now I was aware that I could not stop drinking. This was fine, because I did not want to stop. But it did cause problems. I was a far heavier drinker than most of my friends from university, and certain of them began to shun me. My wife, Peggy, left on two or three occasions. Each time I would straighten out and tell myself, and her, that I would stop drinking.

After *Blood Ties* was finished, Peggy and I left for Europe. I felt alienated among the other Canadian artists and writers

I met there. I was not the kind of liberal that was in vogue in the seventies; my work seemed to be in direct opposition to the communal spirit of the time, which I felt was bogus. Drink protected me from these ideals I could not take seriously, while hiding my belief in a kind of individual anarchism. I could hide in the bottle, and there was always another bottle after that. Drink let me pretend to be like others while the whole course of my life cried out for me to be something else.

Back in Canada, Peggy decided we must do something about my drinking. So we tried the geographical cure. She picked a spot on the map and we went there, literally to the other side of Canada—Victoria.

We rented an apartment, bought a card table from the Salvation Army. I set up my typewriter and went out for a walk. This was the first of many "walks" in which I would disappear from home, sometimes for days—drinking. Every time I told myself that I would have only one drink. But of course that never happened. The first drink led to more and more. I would start for home but never make it. After I'd been on an almost continuous seven-month drunk, we headed back to New Brunswick. I had completed one story in all that time. I believed I was washed up as a writer, and many of my writing friends were available to tell me this was so—because if you make your name young, like Billy the Kid, there is a price on your head.

It would take well over three years to write my next book,

Lives of Short Duration. During this time Peggy and I moved again, to the worst place possible for me—our hometown.

The blackouts became regular. Each time I drank there would be hours, even days I could not remember. I would start to work and manage to get three pages done. Then, thinking three pages was a wonderful amount, I would go to the bookshelf where I kept my bottle of rum and have one drink, then two. I would leave the house before Peggy got home from work. The night stretched out before me, and many times the next day.

We went back to Europe. For a while Peggy tried to keep up with my drinking. She would sit with me sometimes, and we'd drink through the night. But one night would never do it for me. So Peggy would go to bed, and I would find myself at the bar at nine in the morning drinking beer. Of course, beer was nothing more than piss, so I would drink a few and then buy rum.

I decided that a three-day drunk was nothing to be ashamed of. After all, I was a writer—and all the writers whose work I cared for drank. All the writers I *knew* drank, in fact, and I was younger than most of them by ten or twenty years.

At a point in my life when I had begun to drink alone in earnest, Peggy provided me with the twenty questions. Answer three in the affirmative and you are an alcoholic, she said. I checked yes to nineteen out of twenty. The only one I did not answer yes to was "Does alcohol cause problems between you and fellow workers?" Of course not. I had no fellow workers.

Yet now, when I really wanted to stop, when I prayed to be able to drink normally, I could not. Nor could I control anything I did or said once I started drinking. It was a terrible feeling, not to know what was to happen to me once I went outside. Three-day drunks became three-week drunks, and then three-month drunks.

I would return to my wife and my study in tremors, filled with remorse. I would look at my manuscript in progress and realize I hadn't put a word to paper in weeks. I would, as my sister-in-law once told me, literally stink of booze. I would remember snatches and snippets of conversation, realizing that I had been somewhere, had spoken about something. The words would come at me, pierce my skin like bullets. I would remember railing and ranting at someone—perhaps a friend—and then I would hear that I had threatened someone, or someone had threatened me.

I would vow not to drink again.

I lay on the couch, holding a Bible in my hand (I'm still not sure why), and drifted in and out of horrors. I almost always saw dragonflies flying about the room. I would hear my name being called, and I would sit up, sweat pouring off me, waiting for an intruder who never came.

After a few days, with some proper food and rest, the shaking and the itching would go away. The demons would recede. I would go back to work for a day or two. Then, seeing my chance (an argument with Peg or something else), I would go downtown once more, sure that I would only have a drink or two and be home in time for supper.

But from the time I was twenty-three, a drink or two never happened. Worse for me was the fact that certain people believed I wrote terrible things about the Miramichi. The idea many had was that I sent Peg out to work so I could drink and write "dirty books." They were right about one thing—I had earned no money in years.

I had descended pretty much into hell. It took a long while to get out, for a writer is a strange beast, and so many of my plans revolved around drinking. Drinking is good for the creative mind, I told myself. Drinking liberates you from the mundane and the pedestrian. Drinking is a brilliant man's weakness. Those who don't drink are uninspired, callow cogs. Better dead than becoming one of those artificial, church-going, gossip-slinging mannequins.

One by one those vague absolutes had to disappear. But they were hard to get rid of. I wrecked our car and did not rid myself of them. I was thrown in jail and they did not loosen their hold upon me. My friends turned away from me. Still my central idea of drink as romantic and inspirational continued.

My greatest fear of all, of course, was failure. I could do nothing else in life but write. How, then, could I face up to failure as a writer? Bad enough to face up to being a failure as a husband or a human being. But as a writer, like poor Scott Fitzgerald, you could still be called a *brilliant* failure. If

I chose to quit drinking, I would have no crutch to fall back on when I failed. And by the time I was thirty, everything pointed to my failure.

That idea, compounded by the feeling that my drinking friends were the wisest and most brilliant people I knew, put me in a Catch-22. If I quit, what would they say about me? Did I want them to talk about me as a teetotaller? Never. For what had I said about teetotallers myself? Yet weeks would go by and no friend would call. And in my house, bottles were hidden for those occasions when the demons visited.

The December I was thirty-one, swollen up to 189 pounds, I borrowed a thousand dollars from the bank for presents. I did not buy one present. I bought cocaine and rum and beer, and I started to drink and snort coke midway through the month. Christmas had never been a particularly joyous occasion for me. Worse, my new book, *Lives of Short Duration*, had arrived, and I hated the cover. I was frightened of the pending reviews. I was also bothered by the fact that Peg had bought us skis that year. How could I ski with a bad leg? I couldn't. What would people say when they saw me trying? Better to get drunk and stoned and forget it. Or to go skiing drunk and high on coke. I could always write about it later.

Peggy celebrated Christmas alone, went to midnight mass by herself.

On Boxing Day, my rum and cocaine gone, I sat at the kitchen table with a case of beer, nursing a hangover. Everything in our house seemed desolate. Then Trapper, a friend I had not seen in months, came to the door. He sat on one side of the table, Peg on the other. I sat in the middle, piling beer into myself, looking at both of them.

I had never thought of AA. And when Trapper started speaking to me about it, I had exactly the same feeling that many others have had—what in hell does this guy know about life compared to me?

The thing was, he didn't say he knew more about life than me. He just said: "You're using booze to fight booze—you hit the bottle, it will always hit you back."

Then he said he had been sober for three months. Three months was an eternity. I looked at him and almost laughed. I didn't believe him.

"How in hell did you stay sober for three months?"

"Just come to a meeting," he said.

"You want me to go to a meeting?" I asked Peg.

"I think you should," she answered.

That too was surprising. I had thought she would say, no, you're not that bad yet.

So I told him I would go—but that I wanted to go there the back way. There must be a route we could take where no one would see me? But what was worse, the meeting was that night. He told me he would come and get me at a quarter to eight.

It all seemed too much too soon. For the rest of the day I tried to find some way out. I blamed Peg for getting me into it. But that day I could not get sober and I could not get drunk. I was stuck in no man's land. At quarter to eight Trapper arrived, and I angrily left the house with him.

I had passed the building we arrived at two thousand times without knowing it was an AA hall. But from the first words of the first speaker at my first meeting, I realized that someone else had felt all the things I had, and had done most of them himself; and I felt at home.

I went to AA every second day. I did not drink for one whole month—the longest I had been sober since I was fifteen. Then I went to Ontario on a reading tour. In Ottawa I decided to have a glass of wine. Peggy asked me not to. Don't be ridiculous, I told her. I had not had a drink in a month, and one drink would not hurt. I picked up the wine. I looked at it. I closed my eyes as I drank it. It was seven o'clock on January 26. I would not draw a sober breath until April.

As before, the demons came back. But for some terrible reason, now they were ten times worse—just as the people at AA had told me they would be. Feeling there was no hope, I decided I would drink until I died. I went for drives dead drunk, closing my eyes for snatches of sleep while doing sixty miles an hour. I would wake up in strange places, drive a hundred miles for a drink at a bar where no one knew me. The drunk went on and on and on. It was a deadly drunk in which I tried to kill myself and threatened to kill others. I snuck about town at night, kept myself hidden all day. I drank and did coke with abandon. Finally I found myself at the hospital door, dropped off by someone I had been drinking with. When they started to admit me, I, ashamed and scared, balked and went home.

The house was empty. It was desolate as always. We had not bought a new piece of furniture in years, because I drank up almost everything. Peggy was at work, and the humming of the fridge almost drove me catatonic. So I telephoned Trapper. Once again he came, 220 pounds of muscle and a sweet smile on his face. I remembered how he and I and another friend had gone on weeklong benders, how we had arrived in the Gaspé in a hearse, and how I had thrown a knife though the foot of our drinking buddy. I remembered how Trapper, on a binge, had taken a taxi to Newfoundland, how he had knocked a man cold for a drink of wine. He had once been one of the toughest men on the river. That night he sat down and watched me as I paced the floor. I couldn't sleep, couldn't eat, couldn't do anything but shiver, hot and cold, seeing shadowy figures and hearing my name called. The horrors went on and on. I looked and felt like a man on the way to the gallows.

"Think you'd like to go to a meeting?" he said.

I went back to AA. It was April 2, 1982. I thought people would feel superior to me. But when I walked in, people smiled at me and shook my hand. I hung around. But it wasn't easy. It wasn't easy at all. Sometimes it still isn't. It took months before I felt human, and three years before I was able to complete another book. But since then I have written ten more. Since then, by luck and by God, and though I have been sorely tempted, I have never taken another drink.

BLACKOUT

SHERI-D WILSON

Narcotics cannot still the tooth,
that nibbles at the soul.

—EMILY DICKINSON

WITH A FINAL gesture of good-bye, and my ten-speed tightly secured to the roof of my old Olds, I ran off in 1982 to join the circus maximus poeticus. Among language contortionists and red-nosed clowns, my high-flying aerial act would become legendary from town to town as the Sheri-D Show.

I suppose the whole notion of the Sheri-D Show was conceived on an airplane from Toronto back to my hometown of Calgary when I was seventeen. An older gentleman sat in the seat next to mine. He asked me what I did. I told him I was a poet, and I asked him what he did. He told me *he* was a poet. Sure, buddy, I thought. Don't you know that poets don't really exist? And if they did they wouldn't be on a flight to Calgary? Aren't you a little old to be making up impressive dream professions on airplanes? Turns out he really was a poet, though, a well-known one. At that age, all I could do was dream, in my imaginary circus tights, that somehow my lie, my fantasy, my imaginary me would one day come into being.

I wasn't going to be the goody-goody bunhead from Calgary, Alberta, who married, had kids, and dreamed of all the things she might have seen and done. Oh no. I was going to go out into the world and do something different. I would be the outspoken girl who said and did everything. I would be the one who smoked and drank and swore and did drugs and had wild sex and wrote poetry and made jazz till dawn like the women I had read about. My behaviour would not be limited by my gender. Somehow, I was going to reinvent myself from a sweet, starry-eyed, working-class small-town innocent into an irreverent, well-travelled, well-read, exotic, free-spirited jazz poet. I'd be the dame who'd outdo any man. Drink them under the table in a rally of hilarity, vulgarity and intellect of light-speed and bullwhip slash. The only question was how.

My transition from bunhead to bard began when a friend suggested I attend acting school. Since I had no money, university entrance or other modus operandi, that is what I did. At acting school, the excitement of literature entered the skeleton of my being, making me vibrate with tintinnabulations of euphoric discovery. It was as if all the acting students were coming to life together, and the world stood before us like a big ripe Bing cherry. I would attend classes dressed as Mata Hari or Patti Smith or Virginia Woolf and deliver long diatribes of invented bravado.

One Saturday night I walked across the 10th Street bridge en route to Ten Foot Henry's, the hip hot spot for Calgary's late-seventies alternative art crowd, with the elongated stride of my nineteen years. The Mistress of Wintriness snapped her subzero fingers and the river steamed in hoarer on the verge of shape-shifting into a standstill. My feet moved in sync with my impatience to party, almost percolating a permafreeze tap dance along the glass-glaze runner of the sidewalk. When the secret door to Henry's opened, a blast of warm air and loud music came cascading out onto the street, sweet as a long swoon. I paid my cover, and I was off to the rampage. Postdisco inferno on a Dionysian night. Nothing could stop my strut. I drank shooters from my body flask for the feeling of contraband inebriation. Smoked Cheech and Chong spliff, and snorted lines as long as Molly Bloom's soliloquy from oversized purse mirrors in toilet stalls. Bodies snaked sensual as a belly dancer's undulation around the curves of beatitude, free love, passionate poetry and R&B loud enough to boom through my bones like a Goliath timpani. There were madcap projections of art on the walls, couches downstairs for the greenroom-cool and me and the band. Everyone seemed to have a flair for the unacceptable. This was the scene. I was in it—and I was out of it. Totally. I remember someone handing me a joint, and then there was... a *Cat on a Hot Tin Roof* click, and then there was... spinning, and then there was... nothing. I don't remember the river that took me home that night, but somehow that's where I ended up.

The next afternoon I was in the bathtub dreaming of the South Seas, looking deeply into the postcard of the Cook Islands taped, with curling corners, beside the four-legged tub. Every hue of tropical blue was trying to distract me from a metal-bending headache when my roommate knocked. "There's someone here for dinner."

"Okay, I'll be right out," I bellowed, before whooshing underwater. I didn't have any idea who was coming for dinner. Blub, blub, blub. I hadn't invited anyone. But the doorbell kept ringing and ringing. When I finally dressed and entered the living room there it was, an octopus with a bottle in each arm—eight men and eight bottles of wine. Not bad for a girl who couldn't get a date in high school. A scene from *Twenty Thousand Leagues under the Sea*, happening in my own living room. May the best sucker win, I remember thinking, may the best sucker win.

I squeezed myself out of the headlock/bottleneck by phoning a few girlfriends, ordering oodles of pizzas, and having a really good time. Later I heard a joke about being invited to my house for dinner. I felt like an urban myth. The first time I had pulled the roulette trigger of blackout obliteration, I had become a legend in my own time. Suddenly I was Dorothy Parker at the Algonquin, Charles Bukowski in female form. I had instantly become eccentric and mysterious, with a Patti Smith–like contempt for the dangerous. I'd dared to sample the bite-sized hors d'oeuvres of blowfish and lived to talk about it. The Sheri-D Show had premiered.

After acting school, I became interested in alternative approaches to the craft. I auditioned for a West Coast theatre that worked with the Odin technique, and I was hired as a company member. In Victoria I met people who took a vested interest in my education, and I realized the best way for me to learn was to find my own teachers/masters. Theatre was the perfect place for me to unravel writing through continual analysis of text and character. I was hungry for new perception, and I started writing my own texts. After my contract with the company expired, I moved to Vancouver, where I began performing my writings in galleries, living rooms and clubs: anywhere they'd listen to me. I met people from the same mind-tribe everywhere. After my first performance piece, *Tight Wire*, was performed in 1983, the Melmoth Group (West Coast surrealists) asked me to join them. It was a huge turning point in my educational process, like being given the gift of new eyes.

In the late eighties poetry entered my life for real. I was twenty-eight when I attended Naropa (the Jack Kerouac School of Disembodied Poetics) in Boulder, Colorado, as a noncredit student. The first night, I went to the opening dance, and before I knew it I was totally ripped. Everyone else split early because they wanted to meditate in the morning, but I was still on fire. I thought I was going to explode with excitement. On my way home I suddenly imagined I was in a musical. There I was, performing a beatnik song-and-dance number down the middle of the street, running and jumping and howling like Kerouac in *Dharma Bums*, flying through the air singing at the top of my lungs. And then, somewhere in the middle of the ecstatic air, I hit a streetlamp shadow and couldn't see the ground below. There was a split second when I felt everything go out of sync. And then I heard my ankle snap. I screamed blue murder, but there was no one around to hear my yowl as I dragged my poor foot home behind me, whimpering like an injured dog. The next day I went to the hospital and got the inescapable cast and crutches. I couldn't believe it. There I was at a Buddhist university with a broken ankle. Everyone gave me that someone's-telling-you-to-slow-down look. And I gave them my I-know-I-know-I've-got-a-lot-to-learn look back. But it amazes me how long it actually took me to see the connection between dying and death.

I will never forget the curse of triumph that rushed through my veins when Anne Waldman pronounced "You're a poet." I had been ordained by the Holy Mother of Poetry herself. It was happening. I was starting to live inside my own dreamscape. Studying, meditating, attending readings and lectures, and partying with my lifeline idols: ringmaster Anne Waldman, poetry high priestess Diane Di Prima, white clown Allen Ginsberg, torch-song juggler Peter Lamborn Wilson, cannon-blasted daredevil William S. Burroughs, set designer David Hockney, ring announcer Marianne Faithfull, and organ grinders Michael McClure and Ray Manzarek. I was the great trapezist Martini partying with the crème de la crème of the big top. This was the cirque de la scène for the party elite, and I was part of it. My dreams of aerial acrobatics were manifesting. I wanted to go higher, with no safety lines. I wanted to breathe fire, juggle chain saws, and tame wild tigers with whips and chairs. At the same time, it hit me on the head like an anvil that to become an artist would take a huge amount of work. For the first time I felt the weight of the slippers I had chosen to wear.

A few years later I was in Toronto at a massive early-winter theatre fund-raising booze-schmooze. Everyone was decked out in true eighties Toronto style, black leather jackets adorned with cock rings to look tough, with just enough colour to appear New York City–smooth. There was hair everywhere except on the skinheads. I was surrounded by gazillions of glamazons I hadn't seen for eons, and we were all in high form, having a blast, talking and dancing and flirting and laughing. We were the Warhol scene of our time, goddamn it. Someone gave me a strip of free drink tickets, and I was off.

I had just toured eastern Canada with Marianne Faithfull and Barry Reynolds, then checked out their concert/recording at St. Ann's Church in New York City, and I felt the cachet of my NYC swish as I regaled small groups of artists with stories of my latest exploits. The Sheri-D Show was in full swing. I'd learned that all a rapturous anecdote required was the resin of truth and a witty punchline. My life could sound as interesting as I wanted, and booze helped me exaggerate my trendy fairy tales to mythical proportions.

After a while I stepped outside and found the perfect spot for fresh air and a cigarette under a wrought-iron fire escape. The booze was playing pick-up sticks with my head. Halfway through my smoke a wild-looking woman joined me. She didn't look like the other partiers; she was older, harder and closer to the streets. She had enough street smarts to devastate any New York City swarm, I thought to my drunken self, in her black matted fur, with her pointed rat-woman nose. She *was* theatre, the real thing, and the people inside were merely impersonators. I was already ripped, but when she reached her short, dirty fingers into her breast pocket and revealed a fatty with the revelation of a master magician, I couldn't say no. One drag and I felt the familiar Tennessee Williams click. I promised to go by her studio sometime... click... click... click... This rat could sniff out the darkest hiding spot in any sewer. She ruled the place where cats got lost and never returned. Top rat to Nosferatu. Queen of the Underground. She scared the living shit outta me. I took one last puff, and I was out of there. Poof.

Riding a rat-tail undertow back to the party, by now in full underwater swing. Breaking everyone moving in slow motion   between strobes   popping   echos enlarged across synchronized sea floor lights bending into nautilus boomerangs   coloured slur red mouths laugh in wide ruby scales eyes closed in blue eyeshadow   Scotch   another Scotch lights hit a sea of dancing leather   infrared rat eyes laser through studs   flicker. Suddenly everyone's leaving. Put on coat   stand outside. Shiver   follow rat-woman   cram into cab   body-parts   elbows   backs of heads   tails   bending arrive somewhere   spill out of car. Air bites my skin with a cold-blooded shark's tooth.

Inside there's a studio   with all these bicycles hanging upside down. Hundreds of bicycles   rafters of bicycles millions and millions of spokes   a sky of wheels. Man Ray's dream home. Fellini's. Loud music. Lines and lines and lines on mirrors. I notice squid eyes staring. Who'd she come with? I can hear them think. They all hate me. Smell a rat. Time to make a break. Outside stars in snowlights. Lonely. Somewhere. Walk. Walk. Door slightly ajar, go in, lie down, close eyes.

I woke in the early morning, sick as a dog, lying on somebody's couch still dressed in my coat and boots and black velvet hat. Whose house was I in? What city? No idea. No sign of life. I tiptoed out. Around me the smells of Toronto's Kensington Market opened, the bustle of bazaar stirred. I hailed a cab and went back to the place where I was staying. My friends served me packages of chicken noodle soup to help my electrolytes as I pieced together a poem of the night. "Pissed as a Sewer Rat," I called it.

I was becoming as addicted to the Sheri-D Show as I was to the booze. Somehow the two went together. I was completely absorbed by the constant chaos, the shenanigans, word quips, poetry and troublemaking that would unravel around me when I drank. I was the social epicentre of hilarity, my adventures side-splitting anecdotes I would later use in my writing. Everyone seemed to love the half-cut Sheri-D. Back in Vancouver, I did poetry readings for a small fee and an unlimited bar tab. Wasn't that how poets were supposed to act? The way I saw it, the more I drank, the more money I was making. And the more calamity and danger I experienced, the more I desired, like going deeper and deeper into a subterranean city of the unknown. If my work was going to reflect my life, as my life reflected my work, everything had to be taken to the cutting edge. I didn't want to be seen as a fake, which meant I had to be the real thing. A sense of risk dominated every episode of the Sheri-D Show. It was reality TV before its time. My body could barely withstand the strain I was putting on it with one death-defying act after another. But luckily, I had a dancer's stamina and discipline. No matter how bad I felt, I never stopped doing my work.

The nineties came in with a bang. I had my first play professionally produced, my second book was published, and I was travelling extensively doing poetry readings and performance pieces. Life had never looked so good. I was back and forth between Lotusland and the Big Apple so much I felt like a flea in a windstorm.

When a close friend suggested I "be careful" with my drinking, I thought her ridiculous. How could I give up drinking? It was a crucial part of who I was. It had become part of my identity as an antimaterialist neo-beat poet. Sheri-D the drinker was invited everywhere, because people loved the madness that ensued. That Sheri-D was in big demand.

What would she do next? Just wind her up with a few cocktails and watch her go crazy. And I *was* crazy, completely nuts, experiencing blackout after blackout.

I attended a poetry retreat in the mountains. Poets from all over North America had gathered to do readings and share ideas. The drinking began early and ended late. After a dance where we'd consumed enough alcohol to capsize a large oceangoing vessel, a poet friend invited me to come back to his room to smoke a joint and listen to music. We'd been chatting for about half an hour when there was a knock at the door. He yelled, "Just a minute." Then he turned to me and whispered, "As I was leaving the dance, a large woman asked if she could come back to my room and have sex."

"So?"

"That must be her."

"So?"

"Go into the bathroom and hide."

"That's stupid. I'll just leave."

"No. She can't know you've been here, 'cause then you'd know she'd been here."

For some strange reason this made sense to me, and the next thing I know I'm in a dark bathroom, pissed and stoned to the gills, with my ear pressed to the door. I hear him let her in, and then he returns to the bathroom, runs the tap, and gives me my next set of instructions. "Okay, I'm gonna go out there, and when we start doin' it, you tiptoe out of the room without her seeing you."

"Are you fucking crazy?"

"Please, just do it, for me, please."

"Okay, okay, okay. God!"

He turns off the tap, and once again I'm standing in a dark bathroom wondering how I got myself into this; better still, how I am going to get myself out. Within minutes I hear them getting it on. I opened the door a crack to peek, and I couldn't believe what I saw. My friend was completely buried under the largest naked woman I had ever seen. She was so enormous her body actually rippled over the sides of the single bed. I opened the door a little wider. She was riding him like a great white elephant on top of a mouse. I hoped he was still alive under there. I eased slowly out of the bathroom. As I slinked along the wall, I could see small pieces of him, reaching out from behind the flab, and he was making bold gestures pointing me in the direction of the door. I smiled at him in defiance and stood there watching in total disbelief. Then I tiptoed across the room, licked my fingers, and I stuck them up the fat girl's ass. Just like that. She jumped with excitement, turned her huge body slightly back, smiled, and continued riding the mouse-poet. Obviously I hadn't thought this one through! What do you do when you've got your fingers stuck up a fat girl's ass? Where do you go from there? What do you say? I slapped her vast white butt a few times and then I withdrew my phallus-fingers and I flew, out the door and down the hall. I was frantic. I couldn't believe what I had just done, but it made me laugh in wild bursts of madness. There was loud music and voices at the end of the hall, so I ran in that direction. Out of breath, feeling like a cartoon character, I screeched into the room. And then I acted nonchalant, as if nothing had happened. The poets welcomed me, handed me a joint, and I sat down splat, already composing a poem entitled "I Stuck My Finger up the Fat Girl's Ass."

I wanted to be the Dorothy Parker of the nineties. I wanted to be the witty, foul-mouthed poetess, with a cigarette in one hand and a martini in the other, soaked in single malt, stirred. But my face was beginning to run like a sad clown's.

In 1997, after a reading in Seattle, I met F. He was interested in poetry and in visiting Canada from the United States of America, so we kept in touch for six months, and then he decided he'd come up for a visit. I made it clear that he could stay for five days tops, so when he arrived and announced that he'd booked his airplane ticket for a twelve-day stay, I felt more than slight aggravation. I had made it equally clear that I was not interested in any intimate interaction, so when he crept into my bedroom in his unwashed boxer shorts the second night of his stay, I was the antithesis of impressed. After three days I was irritated with F.'s whining, bloodsucking and neediness to the marrow of my organism, even imagining ways I might waste the fucker in his sleep.

One of my oldest friends called and invited me to a party. When I told him about my irritating houseguest he laughed and said, "Bring him along." F. was certain he wouldn't like any of my friends, so I dropped him off at a local pub where he could play darts instead. He'd meet me at the party later.

Surprise! It was an engagement party, my worst nightmare. The host, who had made a "never marry" pact with me twenty years previously, was suddenly tying the knot with a bleached-blonde trophy twenty years his junior. The party was jam-packed with dull-brained gold-digging blondettes and beer-bellied divorcés uptight about their steep alimony payments. And with bottles of expensive single-malt Scotch.

"Sure. I'll try the rarest first." "Sure, pour me another." My friend announced his engagement with a toast. "Sure, I'll have another." "Sure." How could he break the blood-oath we had made all those years before? We were going to live differently from the rest of the world, he and I, but here he was joining the legions of mediocrity without even forewarning me of his twisted proposal. "Yeah, I'll have another. Make it a triple." My mood was definitely on the rocks.

On my way to the bathroom, I overheard one of the bimbettes telling a prospective husband that she would never have sex before she was married. Bat, bat, bat. Before I had time to think, I turned on my heel and blurted out, "You were a teenaged slut, for Christ's sake, it's written all over you. And now you'd fuck anything that moved for the promise of a ring and a bank account with unlimited credit." The party stopped. I smiled smugly, then retired to the can. As I sat down I noted that (1) I was the only brunette at this saturated soirée, and (2) Maybe I'd gone too far. I giggled to myself. Oh, what the fuck. Flush.

Turns out that little Miss "I'd Never Have Sex Before I

Was Married" was the bride-to-be's best friend. Oops. But her prospective husband, enchanted by my swish frankness, invited me to join their group conversation. The blonde gaggle cut an enormously wide berth to accommodate my atrocious mouth. The Scotch had taken hold and I was on a rampage. I held court, telling live sex stories until my friend asked me to leave the party.

Just then F. appeared at the door. On our way outside he grabbed my car keys from my hand. I was incensed, and my late-night visions of murder rose to the surface, but I let him drive. As we passed a corner store, I suggested we stop for cigarettes. "Why don't you come in, and we'll buy some munchies?" I said to F. sweetly.

Once inside, I took the opportunity to punch F. in the head, right beside the potato chips. As he was falling, I grabbed my car keys and cut out of the place. Taking back roads to avoid interference, I drove straight to a friend's place. There was a small group gathered there, and I had them in stitches within seconds.

When I got home the next morning, there was a message from F. He had called the police, who had given him a ride to the airport, and he was thinking of charging me with assault. I phoned him back with a reply threat. My F.U. finger had been broken by the punch, his clothes were already in the dumpster, and I was not in the mood to negotiate.

Three rings in the circus of self-hate, and the circus was getting wilder. I felt beat-up half the time. It was as if I was running behind myself, trying to catch up, calling my own name. "Sheri-D! Wait up!" I was out of breath. Tired. The circus was a nightmare. A blur. Ta-dah! The Sheri-D Show had won, and the real Sheri-D was dead. The blackouts were now so close together there seemed to be no space between them. I had become a sideshow act pierced and branded from head to toe.

I knew by now that my drinking was out of my air-traffic control, but I didn't know how to put myself out of my misery. I knew I wanted the noise to stop, but I couldn't locate the stereo. There had been a time when I had control over the alcohol, and then there was a turning point when alcohol took control over me, completely. Initially the blackouts had happened only when I was drinking. But I had started having gaps in consciousness even when I was sober. Everything had become muted and distorted, as if I were living underwater.

One of my last full-on drinkathons occurred in Montreal. All I remember of that trip is arriving with several thousand dollars and leaving with none. After I quit drinking I ran into several people who saw me at that time, but I have no recollection of them or of the events. One of those people, a poet friend, was still horrified when I bumped into him a year later. He said he'd had to leave the party during my binge-fest in Montreal because he couldn't watch me any more. He told me he'd actually wept. He couldn't bring himself to tell me what he'd witnessed and, to tell the truth, I didn't want to know. When you're playing blackout roulette, it's difficult to remember how many clicks there've been. How many blanks does the gun hold?

I'll never forget that Father's Day morning in 1999 when I woke up with the taste of poisonous disgust in my mouth. I don't know why it happened that way, on that particular morning, but it wasn't the hangover I felt sick from that day, it was myself. That morning I felt shame for who I had become. I knew I was in big trouble, and I felt ugly to the core. My life no longer seemed humorous or intriguing. I was utterly sick of being sick: sick of puking my guts out into a pail beside my bed every second night; sick of crawling up the front stairs of my building and sleeping on the landing 'cause I couldn't make it to my door; sick of apologizing for things I couldn't remember I'd said and done; sick of the massive phone bills for late-night drunk-o-logues; sick of the excuses and the accidents and the ambulances. But most of all, I felt sick of being someone I wasn't. I was sick of the Sheri-D Show. I wanted to go back to being that crazy eccentric kid from Crocus Road who imagined she was Emma Peel as she played kick the can. That morning I made the commitment to myself that I would stop drinking and start down the slippery path of recovery.

I kicked the physical addiction first, which felt like giving birth to myself. Literally, out of my own asshole. I spent a lot of time walking to release the pain. Now I'm working on the psychological recovery. At times I feel lost, as if I don't know how to do things any more, as if I don't know who I am. At those times, I slow down and remind myself to listen. When I stopped drinking I started to live again, and when I started to live again I started to remember some of what I had forgotten. Vulnerability is difficult for me after playing the been-there-done-that tough girl for so long. I was worried I'd become soft when I quit and have diddlysquat to write about. As it turns out, the incidents in my life are even more out of the ordinary, with deeper resonance, and now I always have the energy to write.

Finally, I have goosebumps again. For a long time they atrophied, along with the rushes, the surges, the peaks and the valleys. But now they've resurfaced, and the curve of a burnt tree against the sky on a walk along the river, the sound of an undiscovered word, the pause of a deep song all move through me as pure sensation. Sometimes it feels as if my head will blow off. As if I'm being hit by lightning bolt after lightning bolt. Currents rush through me, and I am struck with ekstasis. Without knowing it, that is what I had been looking for all along.

In 2000, the Vancouver writers' festival had a special tribute to the honourable poet P.K. Page. The afternoon was filled with writers telling stories about their associations with Page, most of which involved drinking antics. It wasn't until the poet herself took the stage that the magic was triggered. Standing there in all her elegance and grace, the emerald ring on her walking-stick hand glittering, she read her poetry with the command of a lioness, never raising her voice. A certain alchemy saturated the space, and her words and sounds entered every molecule of my body and soul and mind and heart and I felt as if the top of my head was peeling off my skull. I was worried I might lose my hair with that much energy surging through! I thought I was going to explode on the spot, and I started to shake. As tears rained down, I felt like I needed a drink. There was too much intensity for my body to house. But why bring myself down with booze, I thought, why not experience the fullness of this? That's when I got it—the connection between poetry and love. The circus mask dropped to the ground, and the Sheri-D Show was pronounced dead. I didn't need the image any more. I really was a poet.

MOLESTED CHILD, SO-CALLED SEXUAL SAVAGE

lessLIE

MY EARLIEST CHILDHOOD memory is being taken into a crawl space underneath the front porch of my family's house, having my pants pulled down and sitting on a white-haired man's lap while he played with my penis. Shortly after that, my young aunt locked me in a bedroom with her. As I stood next to the door, hearing someone outside yelling and knocking, my aunt undressed, got into bed, spread her legs, and began masturbating. At forty-one years old, I am only now shedding my first tears over this experience.

One night when I was six, while my mother, grandparents, and aunts and uncles were getting drunk downstairs, a drunken guest made his way upstairs, where my sister and I were sleeping on a bunk bed. I was on the top bunk, and the man came for me first. He unzipped my pants, pulled them down, and began sucking on my penis. After he finished with me, he knelt down and began pulling on my sister's pants. To protect her, I quickly jumped off my bunk to the floor. The man and I stood face to face, and then he walked out of the dark room.

Such experiences were common when my family was drinking. On two occasions, my drunk uncle sneaked into the bedroom where my sister, my aunts and I were and tried to rape my aunts. I pretended to be asleep, but I witnessed their screaming. Once, after my lonely single mother went out on a date, I accidentally walked in on her and the man she was with. She was sitting on his lap as he slid his fingers inside her. About a year later, my grandmother burst into the bedroom where my sister, my mom and I were sleeping. In her drunken state, she said to my mom, "You better watch Les, because he might turn out to be gay." Although I don't discriminate against anyone with a different sexual orientation now that I am an adult, this experience had a profound effect on me. My familial role models also taught me that addiction and demoralization were "normal." My sexually traumatic childhood experiences, coupled with the highly sexualized nature of mainstream culture and the post-colonial realities of living as an Aboriginal person, shaped my sense of sexuality as an adult.

I recall having unusually strong sexual longings and fantasies as a child. I don't know if my brain was chemically imbalanced or if my experiences with molestation as a child miswired my hormones. Either way, I was a child with prematurely lustful feelings. As a teenager, I never acted on my carnal desires. Instead, out of shyness, self-consciousness and insecurity, I relied on pornography, occasional flirtation and masturbation. I didn't lose my virginity until I was seventeen, and I didn't have sex again until I was twenty-five. I was a man filled with latent desires waiting to be unleashed on the world.

After finishing undergraduate studies at university and beginning graduate work, I finally became sexually active. At first, it seemed ambitious to set a goal of "getting laid" once a month. But I discovered there were women who were attracted to me, so I took advantage. After years of pent-up desires and fantasies, I was ready to explode. I became addicted to one of the primal pleasures of humankind.

From then on, I pursued women. Being an artist was my calling, but chasing women was what I did when I wasn't working. My sex addiction fuelled my career, and my career fuelled my sex addiction. My sex life provided erotic inspiration. My lust was my Austin Powers–style "mojo." From certain perspectives, when I looked at Coast Salish art, with all its clean curves, I saw women's bodies. When I saw a woman's naked body, with all its many colors, I felt artistically inspired. Some of the beauty I perceived in having sex with a woman infused my work with anaesthetic experience of pleasure. In the motion of Coast Salish design, I sometimes saw the motion between my body and a woman's body in bed.

I sought profound insights in my carnal experiences as well. When I was deep inside a woman, I imagined I was looking into reality. I wanted my carnal knowledge to lead to artistic knowledge and wisdom. Whenever I used a compass to draft a circle, I sometimes imagined the shape of a woman's breast being formed. A compass piercing the paper or a spindle whorl shaft sliding in a spindle hole was an erotic metaphor for me. I had the word "cum-pussy" in my mind whenever I used a compass. Yet the word "cum-pass" was also in my mind. The pleasure was always fleeting.

I imagined myself to be Bill Breed, breeding with women while painting the image of a naked woman bent over on a drumskin. I struggled to reconcile Picasso's painting of brothel prostitutes, degraded humanity and African masks. I was haunted by ethnographic "research" that viewed the "primitive," non-Western "other" as sexually liberated. As a contemporary Coast Salish artist, I heard many stories of artists who were alcoholics and drug addicts. Sex was my addiction, my vice of choice. As I attained some recognition as an artist, the lines between fantasy and reality got blurrier. I imagined myself a porn star without camera or crew. My sex life inspired my art, and the money I made from my work fuelled my sex addiction.

I was a ruthless player, an addict trying to avoid my conscience. I began to build what I saw as a harem of women locally, then expanded my geographical range. I met women in public and online. In my eyes, I was a "conquered" First Nations man trying to "conquer" women in bed. Some of the anger I felt from being molested as a child subconsciously came into play. My rage at the racism in Canadian and American society, and at the lack of concern for the environment or for any kind of justice, made me feel a degree of misanthropy, and my insecurity with women made me feel a degree of misogyny as well. Some of the women I landed in bed paid the price for every other woman who had rejected me. In my mind, some of the "white" women I had sex with were paying the price for every "white" woman who had racistly rejected me as well. I had sex with a broad range of women: a poet, a journalist, an academic, a former escort turned web designer, a young party girl looking for a father figure and local women known as "jungle bunnies" (a racist term used to identify First Nations people who are alcoholics and who drink in the public wooded areas around reserves). It didn't matter to me who the woman was. At times, I even fantasized I was a handsome Ted Bundy, with sex as my weapon of choice. In those moments, I saw that sex addiction had the potential to be a gateway addiction, with murder being the "next level" after sex could no longer satisfy me. I didn't feel fulfilled unless I had sex with at least one woman a night. My record was four. On nights when I didn't have sex with at least one woman, I felt like a sexual failure.

As a member of what I considered an emerging Northwest Coast First Nations art royalty, I felt I was sexually entitled to women. Since I didn't move to the reserve where I live until I was nineteen, I also felt a strong need to fit into my community. I was not a highly traditional person, a soccer player, an alcoholic or a band office worker. Reckless sex, I thought, might be my key to acceptance. In a reserve community partially demoralized by colonialism, my demoralized sex life gave me a way to feel like I fit in.

My sex life was an obsession. Even while I was in a gallery doing business, I could sometimes not get out of my mind the image of the woman I'd been with the previous night. One of my sex partners, an older blonde, told me that addicts were people who were running away from themselves. But she had me only partially convinced that the observation applied to my behaviour.

Little by little, I let go of my conscience. I tried to ignore that I was using women. I tried to ignore that I was stringing some women along, giving them the hope of being my one and only. I tried to ignore it if someone felt hurt. I didn't care if I fed a woman's alcoholism to satisfy my lust. I took advantage of women's weaknesses to gratify myself sexually. I made a pact with myself that I would do anything for pornographic sex, even if it meant ruining my life or someone else's.

Instead of notches on a belt, I began a lust list, which included the names of all women I slept with. I wondered if having sex with a hundred women was enough. Two hundred women? In my ravenous lust for women, I once joked that I wanted to have sex with every woman in town. As time passed, however, my lust life began to seem absurd and out of control. At times, I devoted more energy to having sex than to actually working as an artist. And, as all addicts know, an addiction starts to lose its appeal over time. Having sex sometimes felt like more of a demanding physical process than a pleasure. When I took the time to look deep into my soul, I realized that I was a menace to society and to myself.

I tried to rationalize my sexual appetite by fantasizing that I was a genius, a self-destructive artist who created profoundly culturally significant work. But eventually, guilt caught up with me. The fear of causing an unplanned pregnancy or of becoming sterile from an undiagnosed STD also haunted me. I could see that my sex addiction was taking a toll on my emotions, my career, my health—and my soul. I am characteristically a shy man, but I spent many nights not being myself, simply putting on the charm to get a woman into bed. I wasted hours, even entire nights, waiting for women to show up at my apartment. On more than one occasion, I felt like a prisoner in my own home. One night, an alcoholic woman who was a sex partner of mine buzzed non-stop on my intercom, phoned me, texted me and finally walked to my back window, calling my name as I lay in the dark in my bed, pretending I wasn't there.

As I walked the streets of my town, I wondered if anybody riding by in a car was calling me a "male slut" behind my back. At times, I carried myself with guilt and shame. I was in constant fight-or-flight mode, ready to take on any man who disapproved of me. I was called homosexual by some, because of my sex-addict strategy of never holding hands with a woman in public. (I always tried to give the impression

I was a shy, good guy who was single.) I was falsely accused of stalking a former date. Another woman, in an attempt to make her husband jealous, accused me of holding her hostage in my apartment. Sometimes after having sex, I would be on the verge of tears, fearing that sex was all that I knew how to do with women, and that I would never have a normal relationship. The women I had sex with ranged from one-night stands who were fleeting pleasures to women I had feelings for. Sometimes I really cared for a woman and her kids, only to leave them behind. That made me feel like I was leaving part of my soul behind with them. I also faced the emotional backlash of women who caught on to my womanizing ways. Still, I tried to ignore the truth and convince myself I was living the fantasy of many men. I rationalized my behaviour by telling those close to me it was biologically programmed into human males to want to have sex with many women.

A burlesque dancer I met online wanted to meet me in person in Vancouver, where she was performing. As I watched her show, I felt that one of my ultimate fantasies was about to be fulfilled. She came to my hotel room, but as always, the pleasure was fleeting, leaving me lonely, empty and longing for my next fix. Once she had dressed and left, I lay alone in my hotel room, crying and asking myself, "Is this all there is for me?" This experience left me longing for real love.

Shortly after this, I met Robynne online. I was expecting just another date to add to my lust list. Robynne was young and pretty and curvy and smart. We had great sex, but she also taught me that love is important. She disapproved of my saying, "Love is dead, long live lust." After my step-grandfather died, a man I loved, Robynne came to my apartment and asked me what I was doing. When I told her I was browsing porn sites, she told me I was not honouring my mourning over my step-grandfather. I got mad, even though I could see truth in what she was saying.

Robynne and I started to feel like a family of two. We both struggled with addictive pasts, though. For her, it was abusive relationships, sex and drinking. And over time, we realized we could not fully let go of our pasts. Even though I loved Robynne, my years of sex with numerous women haunted me. When Robynne and I got into an argument, I invited one of my former sex partners to my apartment. Even though the sex was pleasurable, I quickly regretted it. Robynne forgave me, but later that year, on an exhibition trip to London, England, I met a First Nations woman who invited me back to her hotel. Months later, just before we were set to move in together, Robynne came across the receipt with the other woman's room number and phone number on it. I was caught red-handed. I cried, trying to explain that my behaviour came from my childhood molestation and loneliness. Robynne forgave me again, but finally we agreed to break up. After the most loving and tender year of my life, she left me.

Lost and lonely, I reverted to my earlier ways. I bragged to one of my best friends that I had many more women to look forward to. But the truth was that I was heartbroken. I had to learn the hard way that addiction can cause you to lose those you love most. I no longer wanted to live in my body. Desperate, I decided to commit suicide, and to do it in the most pleasurable way I knew how: by having sex. One of my former sex partners, an alcoholic whose addiction I'd fed, was rumoured to have had sex with one of my cousins, a person living with HIV. As a suicide attempt, I invited this woman to my apartment and had unprotected sex with her.

I was playing sexual Russian roulette. I wanted to end my life, be another tragic story of a brilliant artist whose life ended before it should have. I was full of shame at having been raised by alcoholics who made me live in poverty and got drunk while I was being molested. I felt ashamed of being an "Indian." I was living with the intergenerational legacy of residential schools, the Indian Act and paternalism. I was living with the racist legacy of seeing buff, chiselled, handsome native men embracing white women on the covers of novels and the stereotypes of native women as loose "squaws." Like many of my generation, I was also influenced by the hip-hop image of brown-skinned men as oversexed.

Fortunately for me, I was blessed by meeting another woman who loved me. I met Amanda online, again expecting just another name to add to my list. But over time, I discovered a woman who truly loved me as an artist and a human being. Amanda has been the only family I can rely on when my own family lets me down. She is a loving, compassionate, kindhearted person and someone who cares about perpetuating tradition. Today, she and I are the proud parents of a healthy baby girl. My daughter, Cadence, is a human being in her own right. But she also represents a second chance for me. She is my chance to love and care for a girl right from the beginning of her life. She also gives me a second chance to value, love and respect myself. She is my blessing, my loving inspiration to leave my former addiction behind. Her birth centred me, and her existence gives me a reason to live with pride, dignity and self-respect. My dear daughter brings out the best in me, and I know I can never do anything to hurt her. When she wakes at three in the morning and looks up at me with her beautiful, innocent eyes, I feel connected to the innocent kid inside me.

Recently, I took a walk through a place called Cowen Park with Amanda. It was a healing experience. As a boy, I fled to Cowen Park often to escape the alcoholism, domestic violence, trauma, poverty, and sexual and psychological abuse at home. I would look up at the trees and dream of becoming an artist. On my walk in the park with Amanda, I realized the child I once was is still a special and sacred part of who I am. That innocent boy who dreamed of becoming an artist is with me now, and he will be with me forever.

NOT SWIMMING, BUT DROWNING

JOHN NEWLOVE

I.

It was a soft summer night and I was trying to walk the two blocks home from a wedding dance in the community hall. Men with large trays had been going back and forth, offering glasses of the best local home-brew to all takers.

My particular dance was called one step forward, two steps back, fall into the caragana hedge, puke, rest, and try again. At one point as I was lying in the hedge I heard someone walking. The steps stopped and the corner light shone on a pair of black oxfords. A voice said, “Are you all right?”

I puked on the shoes and they went away.

I got home. Details are vague.

In the morning I woke up lying across my bed, partially undressed, stained with and smelling of vomit. I didn't know if I had been caught or not. My mouth was arid and I had a huge, pulsing, soprano headache.

I loved it. I had found what I wanted. I wasn't John the unlikable, unlovable one. I was that other guy, the tough guy with the same name, but drunk. It was freedom.

That's only the booze talking, people used to say.

Funny stuff; but I don't know any other way to tell you what I am.

I knew this was for me, especially the part about not being able to remember anything.

If you can't remember anything then you can do anything, I thought, and it isn't your fault.

I had been caught, of course. I listened meekly to my mother's reproof—God knows that poor dear woman had enough knowledge of drunks to last an eternity—and agreed with her and said I was sorry and it would definitely never happen again, but absent-mindedly, because I was trying to figure out how to get some more booze.

I was a reasonably bright kid, fourteen, too lazy to do homework but bright enough to read the book the day before the provincial exam and get a decent mark, and I was cursed with an argumentative mind that loved what it thought, in its superior teenage way, was logic.

But it was intuition, not logic, told me that so-and-so (the names have been disguised, as they say, to protect the guilty) was weak. Intuition, not logic, told me that if I kept yapping at him he'd buy me a mickey of rye.

It didn't take much intelligence, logic or intuition to realize that in a town of about two thousand people a fourteen-year-old walking around with a case of beer would be noticed. I didn't consider wine; that was for drinking with fancy meals or on fancy occasions, the novels told me, and in the novels no one ever seemed to get drunk.

I wanted to get drunk. I wanted to get pissed out of my head.

I was right about so-and-so. Evil little bastard that I was, I knew once he'd bought me the first bottle he was hooked. What if I told someone? He got me a mickey of rye on a Friday. Because my parents were going to Yorkton Saturday I saved the whisky till then.

Saturday morning I got up, had my breakfast, and wished and wished and wished that they'd hurry up and go to Yorkton.

After they left I had a big slug of the rye and nearly puked again. Puking was looking like something I could get good at. I couldn't skate worth a damn, to this day I don't know the difference between an in-turn and an out-turn; I couldn't dance, or wouldn't; I still have three small spots of lead in my right hand where Karen stabbed me with a pencil after I tried to grab her largely theoretical tits in Grade 9; and I had a bad mouth and flew into screaming, sobbing rages I could never see coming on and if I got clocked in a fight it didn't matter, because nothing could hurt me.

I would have been one hell of a small-town Saskatchewan-style defenceman if my skating had been a better.

(Oh Karen, lost, never realized darling I was so afraid of, I asked about you in 1980 and they told me you were fat, and this isn't even your real name.)

Once I mastered my gorge I drank the rest of the rye as quickly as I could—it wasn't anything like as good as the local home-brew—and puked on the nasturtiums. I hid the empty mickey in a culvert and walked down to Peter's Pool Palace and breathed on people.

"Jesus, have you got a skinful," one kid said. "Where'd you get it?" "Ask me no questions, I'll tell you no lies," I said. We never actually talked—at least I didn't—but it didn't matter much because none of us trusted closeness and we had an encyclopedia of pat phrases designed to push people away.

When my parents came home in the early evening it was obvious I'd been drinking. My mother gave me The Look and went into the front room to confront my father.

"Harold," she said, "you've got to talk to that boy."

"What can I say," he said.

He was a drunk too. He was a man I remember seeing only on odd occasions, briefly, before I was ten, in three of the small Saskatchewan towns where my mother taught. My guess is that my mother loved him dearly but wouldn't put up with his drunkenness; attempts at living together must have failed many times.

In Veregin, when I was in Grade 4, my mother was the principal of the local two-building, three-room public and high school. My father had set up a new law practice in Kamsack, nine or ten miles away. He lived there weekdays. On weekends he came to stay in Veregin and whipped the shit out of me.

I knew, or I thought I knew, that I had been an unwanted baby, an accident. I made up stories. I convinced myself that my mother and father had had an earlier child, about the same age as my much older brother and sister, with exactly my name, and that I was just a replacement for him. Because, unlike most of the people I saw, my father seemed to think that Indians were human beings, I convinced myself that I was a Saulteaux orphan they had adopted.

And so on and so on. I couldn't be real. It was clear to me that though I was capable of loving desperately, I myself was unlovable.

There you are. I stood in the high-school gym during sock dances feeling sorry for myself.

At least self-pity is never a false emotion.

One weekend my father came home sober and he never drank again. He'd been to AA and it worked. He was a stubborn bastard. I admired him. I still do. He wouldn't take Communion because he was afraid that even that small taste of wine would set him off.

Much later my mother told me that when she came to my little room in Veregin to kiss me good-night on my father's first sober Saturday I asked her who that man was.

2.

I was registered at the University of Saskatchewan for a year but I had to pass pubs on the way to classes. I had my first draft beer at the Senator. We go grey early in my family and I'd had some grey in my hair since I was sixteen or seventeen: not tragedies, not heartbreak, just genetics. I thought it might get me by.

The Senator had two levels. I went to the top one because there was no one else there, sat down and put a five-dollar bill on the table. My intuitive, intelligent, logical mind had never gotten around to asking anybody what draft beer cost, but I knew five bucks would cover it easily; then I could count the change and figure it out. A bored waiter came over and put two draft on the table. I eased the five-dollar bill toward him. He made change (he'd given me two big glasses, twenty cents each) and I dropped a dime into his hand.

I had a mouthful of beer. I thought, Okay, I can do this any time. I looked around. The waiter was leaning against the wrought-iron railing that divided the lower and upper floors. He was watching me. When he saw that I was watching him too he came over and put my draft back on his tray. I thought, Oh shit. He said, "Follow me," and I did. He went to a two-man (no women allowed) table behind a big pillar, put my draft on it and said, "Sit here, sonny. Nobody can see you here."

3.

Then I had various jobs, for most of which I was not qualified; but one thing you learn early as a drunk is that you've got to be able to talk your way out of any of the shit you've landed in, and that doesn't demand anything but charm. I found out that I could put it on, so I added charm as one more thing on my list of stuff not to trust. In the meantime, I was a high-school teacher, a social worker (public assistance, not a baby snatcher), a continuity writer and announcer for three small Saskatchewan radio stations and, when I couldn't avoid it, a ditchdigger, warehouseman, swamper and general asshole.

I made my voice deep.

4.

My life consisted of one desire only. Get pissed. Get out of it.

"She's a pig, man, and she's stupid, too. How can you do it with her? You got no self-respect, man," a friend said in a beer parlour somewhere.

He was right, but I won. "She buys me booze, man," I said. "You're drinking her money right now."

"Point," he said. "But I'm just glad I don't have to fuck her."

"I'm no prize either," I said. "One of these days I'm going to tell her who I'm pretending it is if she'll tell me who she's pretending it is. In the meantime let's get the hell out of it."

5.

No problem. I could stop right now if I wanted to. No problem. But I don't want to.

6.

Years later in Nelson, B.C., when my wife was away—I think she was away—I did stop.

Before you can go into the addicts' floor in the hospital you have to have been dry for seven days. After the bars had closed I went home and knocked myself out with a forty-ouncer of Ballantine's and whatever beer was around. I collapsed on the chesterfield. When I woke up I drifted off and woke up and drifted off and started to shake and I thought, This is bullshit, I can do this any time. I just don't want to do it now. But it was the middle of the night, as my logical mind had thought it might be, and I didn't know any bootleggers.

When I woke up fully it was because the phone was ringing. I fell off the chesterfield and crawled over to the phone and picked it up. It was my doctor, Liz, and she was worried about me because I'd told her what I was going to try. She'd phoned to tell me that she'd tried to get me a hospital bed so she could sedate me, but no beds were available. One of the loony premiers of British Columbia was busily saving the taxpayers of the province, who at the time included me at a fairly high level, money by shutting down hospital beds.

Liz once said she could not understand how someone as intelligent as I was could do this to myself.

Intelligence has nothing to do with it.

Okay. I was very thirsty and I was starting to have convulsions. I wanted to crawl to the bathroom. I figured I'd be able to turn on the cold-water tap in the bath and slurp up some water like a dog.

Dogs. I couldn't go that way because in the corner blocking me off was a big white St. Bernard with its chest a sheet of fresh wet blood and it was smiling at me. I got to the kitchen instead and managed to spill a package of sugar on the floor and licking it up got my saliva running.

Let me tell you about the medical profession. Never go to a male doctor. The guy who admitted me to the addicts' floor in Nelson gave me a full-blown God-to-a-little-black-beetle moral lecture and then a very rough physical exam, including an anal examination that amounted to a rape.

Rape must be fun if you don't like love, or even sex.

An emergency-room doctor who stitched up my mouth one time told me, when I said to him afterwards, "That wasn't much of a painkiller you gave me," "I never give painkillers to drunks."

Male nurses are more forgiving than females nurses are, though. Female nurses, like male GPs, know that you are doing this to harass them when they've got people who are really sick to look after and you can stop any time you want to stop: it's a moral problem.

Specialists don't matter much because you're just a thing to them.

7.

Clinically, pancreatitis is one result of alcoholism. The pancreas gives up in despair and refuses to process your food. My doctor in Ottawa was English and she weighed me on an old imperial scale. When I got to 134 pounds from 195 she said, "You have a very strong constitution, Mr. Newlove. Why don't you give it a chance?"

I discovered that if you have water handy and some sour-lemon candies to keep your mouth wet, starving to death is a good way to die. You lose interest. You sleep a lot.

A specialist later told me that pancreatitis is very difficult to diagnose, and that what seems like back pain is caused by this little bit of specialized meat spewing out angry juices into the surrounding organs.

Of course, I have back pain on its own.

My English doctor had a total body bone scan done on me—why don't they put television on the ceilings of those cold white rooms for the occasions when you have to lie still for forty minutes?—and she told me I had cracked or broken at least one representative bone in every part of my body, from the right collarbone down.

I said, "I've never broken my collarbone."

"Yes, you have," she said. "See. In two places."

8.

I have seen W sober, but not often. The last time I saw him it was wintertime in Saskatoon and he didn't know what city he was in.

I have never seen X, Y or Z sober.

The last time I saw X we had bailed him out of the drunk tank in the Vancouver Public Safety Building. It had been a close thing but even in the cells he had managed somehow to stay drunk, and now that he was out he was putting a high polish on it.

The last time I saw Y he was being squeezed out a barely open fire door in an Edmonton beer parlour by a very large Cree woman he'd been mouthy to.

The last time I saw Z a friend and I were beating him up at a party. The woman I was with went into the kitchen and told my friend's wife, "John and Mike are beating up Z." Mike's wife said, "Oh, everybody does that."

I have to assume that all four are dead, long dead.

Strange shapes that piss in the night . . .

9.

I'm a drunk and here's one of those not-so-funny riddles about me.

It asks, How can you tell when a drunk's lying?

Answer: His lips move; or his fingers move shakily over the keyboard.

God, I love it.

10.

I think it begins at about age fourteen, give or take a year. I think the child is desperate to be loved, or at least to be noticed. I think the child loves deeply but thinks it is not loveable. I think the child feels it is an afterthought, a mistake.

This child is an only one or is in the situation of an only one. Unique.

Not like the others. Therefore, wrong, hardly human, a performer with no audience, a fake.

It loves its mother and father desperately but nothing they can ever do will convince it that the love is returned.

(Like many young men for a long time I thought I was tougher than I really was, and like many men for a long time I thought I was younger than I really was. I hurt a lot of people I didn't want to hurt, including myself.)

Nothing anyone can do will convince it. It is determined to be a victim.

It doesn't want to be here, to be in this life of pain and shame.

Now I understand who I have been trying to punish all my life, but that is no excuse.

I still don't like to be touched.

II.

When I came downstairs my mother said, "You've been drinking, John."

I said, "They made me do it."

She said, "Nobody makes you drink, John. You do."

My thanks to Lorna Crozier for confirming that the title I have used here was stolen from Stevie Smith. I misremembered the original, which is "Not waving, but drowning."

ONE MORE LAST CHANCE

RICK WHITAKER

IN NOVEMBER 1999 I published a brief essay in the last-page "Lives" column of the *New York Times Magazine*. The piece was headlined "One Last Chance," and in the pull-quote beneath the headline I proudly proclaimed that "Gambling away everything I had—and some things I didn't have—was a quiet act of social rebellion." The essay told of my introduction to poker at a casino in Santa Fe in the summer of 1997; it described a neat arc of quick addiction to the game, the gradual realization that it was an addiction, and my blithe decision to put it behind me after a brief period of abstinence.

Shortly after the article appeared I received a handwritten note in the mail from a woman who worked as a counsellor in an addiction treatment facility. She had written to warn me that, contrary to my cocksure claims in the essay, my addiction to poker was probably far from over. She advised me to treat the addiction seriously and not to assume it would be, or already had been, easy to kick. She was right. It's 2006 and I'm still gambling.

My addiction to poker has persisted for more years than my hero Fyodor Dostoevsky's famous addiction to roulette, which began in 1863 and ended in 1871 after his wife cleverly encouraged him to play. She knew he would lose eventually and would then, as he had before, rededicate himself to writing and so break a long spell of literary silence (and poverty). Dostoevsky quit gambling and wrote *The Adolescent* and then *The Brothers Karamazov*, perhaps the greatest of all novels. It is not unreasonable to surmise that he wouldn't have written either if he hadn't stopped gambling.

I've been talking about my gambling addiction for a long time now. I see a psychoanalyst three times a week, a schedule that's been maintained for nearly five years. His monthly fee is more than my rent. I've put in time at Gamblers Anonymous meetings where I met one guy who said he was a million dollars in debt and hiding in New York from his Chicago "bookies and shylocks," and several women who spent every penny of their disability cheques playing bingo. My boyfriend even went to GamAnon meetings with other gamblers' wives.

Now, at age 37, I consider my addiction to playing online poker to be my single seriously disturbing vice, and there have been long periods in my life when I juggled vices like a clown juggles torches. I've been addicted to a variety of drugs, to sex, cigarettes, vodka, and (when I was a teenager) pinball. I used to sleep all day and stay out all night, which I couldn't do now if I tried. To have just one problem—or one obvious, unnecessary, eradicable problem—is for me an unusually fortuitous condition. I could say I'm almost afraid of giving up poker for fear of having no vice, but the truth is I *want* to be vice-free, and I would therefore like to give up poker. So far, however, I haven't found a way to quit that sticks.

Going into a darkened room alone and playing poker on the Internet against other virtual beings—that is, against presumably real people online—is my most pleasurable and destructive activity. It's akin to masturbation (which has the great advantage of being harmless); its aim, however, is not orgasm but perpetuation. Poker lasts longer than sex, and the chemical reaction it sets off inside me feels better than sex. (I recently looked at pornography while waiting for others in the game to play their hands—I suspect I'm not the first to have thought of doing this—and discovered the two went together very nicely.)

When I am anxious or angry, I can calm myself by remembering that soon enough I will again be alone with my computer, winning and losing, singularly involved in an intricate game that somehow takes my whole emotional and psychic being on a kind of roller-coaster ride, my paltry but sorely needed stake the little red train that flies me so precipitously along the rails. The allure of poker is the heady possibility of outsmarting the other players and thereby taking all their money. There seems no limit to the money one can win; I have turned $20 into more than $1,000 in a few thrilling hours on the Internet, and I've heard stories of college boys regularly making $100,000 a month. It's possible to get rich in a single night of miraculous luck and skill. Very few other arenas in life offer that hope. All you have to do is beat the other players. Every time I play, my intention is to win some money, cash out, and go home. But the more I win, the more I keep winning. Until I lose.

I think of my addiction to gambling partly as a chemically induced, neurological condition, the result of playing poker every night that terrible summer of 1997 in Santa Fe. I gambled, snorted cocaine, and battled for a month with a disabling case of hepatitis, all the while conditioning my brain to release its juices in that certain way that feels so good despite my misery. But like most gamblers, I suppose, part of my addiction is psychological and neurotic: I am hooked on losing. Just the other day I won some negligible sum—$60 or $70—and could not bring myself to go home with that money in my account. I was pressed for time, but I went back to the Web site and within a few minutes had lost it all in a breathtakingly stupid move with a pair of nines.

According to my therapist, I'm re-enacting a scenario concerning my father, who punished me severely on a daily basis throughout my childhood, telling me he did it because he loved me, that it hurt him more than it hurt me. Just a few years ago I learned from my mother that my father always suspected, with reason, that I was another man's offspring. The therapist's interpretation is that as a child I became inured to being beaten and that after it stopped, I subconsciously missed being punished because I believed, deep down, that to be abused was to be loved. I believed my dad (and I believed he was my father) when he said it pained him to hit me, that he did it lovingly.

This hypothesis raises the issue of differing practices in contemporary psychotherapy. Among many approaches there is the newish cognitive behavioural therapy (CBT) that claims, according to the author of an article published in the *New York Times* on St. Valentine's Day, 2006, that "it is not important for patients to return to the origins of their problems, but instead to correct their current 'cognitive distortions,' errors in perception that lead them to the conclusion that life is hopeless or that everyday activity is unmanageable." This contradicts the older, more traditional psychoanalytic method—my therapist's method—which emphasizes a working-out of symptomatic problems based on an analysis of the whole story, going back to childhood, in an atmosphere of free association and interpretation. CBT reportedly works after fifteen sessions; psychoanalysis, in a way CBT's antithesis, helps some people and fucks up others and might take fifteen years to do either.

I am committed to psychoanalysis for a variety of reasons, chief among them that I find it deeply fascinating, but I don't know if it will help me to stop gambling. It hasn't yet. The theory is that once I have uncovered the entirety of my addiction's causes, the addiction will go away. So I keep digging and excavating, but apparently there is something still hidden that sustains its nefarious effect, like a radioactive pellet that undermines the whole landscape. Perhaps my gambling addiction has nothing to do with my father and his compulsion to spank me. But at least, I rationalize, I am putting my addiction to some use by following it, in therapy, to what seems to be the heart of the darkness in my mind. I have considered giving CBT a whirl (I've also fantasized about primal scream therapy), but I'm attached to my old-fashioned psychoanalyst and he assures me we're making progress.

The only physical element that can explain poker's hold on me is the chemical release in my brain, which I can feel and cannot doubt. Some sort of dopamine or whatever it's called is ejaculated into my bloodstream—I'm no scientist, but I know a thrill when I feel one. To achieve this type of pleasure, in my experience, it is necessary to gamble, with money or personal safety or emotional equilibrium or a moral bottom line. Online poker, for me, is the perfect risk, since I do it alone, undistracted. I don't lose too much money at once, and I could win a lot.

Poker is the best of all games. Everybody gets two random cards; what you do with them is up to you; you can win with the worst cards, and you can lose with a pair of aces. You have to be good in order to win steadily, yet even the best players sometimes lose. It's the kind of game you never really have in your pocket—that's what keeps it exciting for hours and for years. You might win six hands in a row at a full table one night and lose every hand until you're "busted" the next. Your opponents collectively form a great, glowering enemy, and you have to summon the courage to take them on without fear or hesitation.

All of this and much more is brought immediately into play for me when I sit down at my computer and log on to a poker Web site. I could easily play poker for eight, ten, twelve, or twenty-four hours a day, endlessly taking on and being beaten by my father, out of love for him and the need for love's evidence, defeat and punishment.

Or perhaps that's just a theory that has very little to do with my need to play poker regularly and often. It seems to be a symptom, in the psychoanalytic sense of the word, but perhaps it's a symptom of my personality rather than of some specific, nameable mental condition or illness. I could choose to white-knuckle it and "get some clean time," as my therapist puts it. But too often the pleasure and satisfaction I derive from playing seems to far outweigh the wholesome virtue of abstaining. It's like a pyschotropic medication: I could go without Prozac and Wellbutrin (both of which I've been taking for years), but why should I go without them if they help me and carry only slight side effects? The Wellbutrin seems to correct the Prozac's dampening of libido, and it also greatly reduces my desire to smoke cigarettes. (I started smoking when I was nine and as an adult used to smoke twenty cigarettes or more per day; I still have strong cravings).

What poker treats in me is anxiety, whether acute or vague, provoked by some specific worry or generated by the mere daily vicissitudes of life. I become anxious every day; I am rarely relaxed. (I think this must be true for most people, perhaps for all who are not well-trained Buddhist monks.) Playing poker gives me a curious mix of stimulation and relaxation—again, like masturbation. Ideally, I play coolly and cleverly, and I win, which feels good; in reality, I get impatient and sloppy, play badly, and lose. But what happens in my brain happens regardless of how I play, whether I win or lose. It's the action that counts, not the money. The excitement—the stimulus—is actually calming, and I am, briefly, relaxed.

Dostoevsky had a theory about playing roulette, that if he played calmly and reasonably, if he could contain himself and not fly out of control, then he *couldn't lose.* When he did lose, he scolded himself that he hadn't stayed calm enough. One of the great minds in the history of the world, the master who wrote *The Gambler*, failed to see that the game itself precludes intelligent play; excitement is its essence, and without it we wouldn't be interested in the first place. Roulette and poker and the lottery and bingo are all poor ways of making money, but they're a lot more fun than working for it. Poker is fun, and roulette clearly was fun for Fyodor.

That is another aspect of the problem: like good drugs, gambling delivers too much pleasure. In this sense poker, for me, is not unlike crystal methamphetamine, a substance that has enabled some of my most memorable highs and misery-ridden lows. Poker and crystal are terrible, wicked temptations for an addict; each has exerted its power to activate something in my brain that was so consoling, so soothing, that it seemed worth the price despite my full knowledge that it was not. What antidepressants do to the brain may well be irreversible and even cause permanent damage. The long-term effects of Prozac have not been studied, because no one has yet been on Prozac for the long term.

As for poker, its side effects are no less than the loss of money, time, and peace of mind. When I'm playing poker, my relationships, my professional life, and my mood all falter. The crippling mental laziness and the paralyzing guilt have a debilitating effect on every good impulse in my life. Poker is amusing but also, ultimately, demoralizing.

If it's been more than a day or two since I last played, I begin to feel a tension that can be quite vague—until I think of poker. The tension leads me to a belief that poker is the only means by which I will be freed. When I give myself permission to play again, I already feel better. Then it's just a question of how soon I can make it happen. Other obligations—to friends, partners, or family, to dinner, shopping, or work—are pushed aside in my head by the undeniable desire to sit alone at my computer, clicking a mouse, winning and losing money. As soon as I'm playing, there's great relief, as if I've returned home after a frightening, exhausting trip to some ugly shopping mall or public event. The game is my friend; it welcomes me back with open arms and a devilish grin that I find irresistibly cozy. I settle in and play conservatively, carefully, like Dostoevsky. Usually I win some hands and increase my bankroll. After a while, the tension inside me softens. I loosen up, play more recklessly, have more fun, enjoy the game. Then I begin to fade—and this is when I should pack up and go home, but I keep playing. I take more risks, seek more action, wake myself up. I play faster, more aggressively, and sometimes this helps my game, and I win more. Inevitably there is a particular hand, which I lose, that initiates my downfall. From there it's smooth sailing until I'm broke.

I have lost many thousands of dollars playing poker. The depressions I fell into afterwards gave my boyfriend excellent reasons to leave me, and if he had, I would have done nothing about it at the time. My second book, much of which was written under the influence of gambling, is plainly inferior to my first, a deeply humbling and humiliating fact that can't be changed. I have been, at times, unable to feel the happiness I could sense to be upon me, a happiness that could vitalize me if only I could drop my resistance to it and overcome the daze induced by endless hands of poker.

For nearly as long as I've been addicted to playing poker I have been very close to a boy, Nico, who is now fourteen, the child of a friend who lives just a few blocks away. I see him almost every day, and I am expected at times to look after him, advise him, protect him, and help him through what may be the most difficult period of his life. Nico is having a typical adolescence characterized by turbulence, rebellion, and sweetness. He is often, I can see, in some emotional discomfort. I'm aware that Nico considers my behaviour—the way he sees me live—to be an example he can choose to follow or swerve away from. What he does with his knowledge of my life is up to him, but the material I give him is the most important thing I have to offer.

Nico copes with the same craving for oblivion and mental ease that I experience in advance of playing poker. When he arrives at my office or apartment after school, he will sit down at the computer without taking off his coat or accepting a glass of water and immediately immerse himself in a game of simulated violence. He fires from airplanes and fights with monsters and rescues girls and flees from the police in fast cars. And truly, he's gone. To speak with him, I have to tear him away from the game, a wrench that is evidently almost physically painful for him, as it is for me when I'm interrupted during a hand. It's clear that, like me, he needs to escape, that he cannot bear to feel his feelings or to be fully himself twenty-four hours a day. He's addicted to playing games on the computer, just like me, one of the few adults in his daily life.

I hide my poker playing from Nico, because I want to be a person he chooses to emulate and admire. But Nico doesn't hide his addiction from me. Instead of playing with the dog or doing his homework or reading a book or talking with me, he fires and fights and drives, his virtual self going through a virtual battle as his real friend stands by, struck silent by the terrible knowledge that we both must find a way to give up what we most want to do. This need to let go of and abandon what feels good is our shared dilemma.

However true it may be that Nico looks to me as one of his role models or at least as one of the decent adults he's close to, it is likewise true that I look to him as a wonderful specimen of humanity. He is the embodiment of resilience, joie de vivre, and possibility. It is perhaps the thought—which I cringe to summon—that he will follow me, even without knowing it, into the mire of addictive behaviour, that is my best weapon in this battle against compulsive gambling. I like to believe I would do anything for Nico. It may be that he requires nothing less of me than a redefinition of love, a banishing of repetitive defeat, and an embrace of the fullness of my singular life.

JUNKIE

STEPHEN REID

THE BLOOD BROKE into two rivulets along the smooth skin of my inner forearm. My head sank back into the new leather of the bucket seat and my body went limp. Paul returned the glass syringe to its coffinlike case and dabbed at my arm with a soft white cotton ball. His face swam up to mine, as if to steal a kiss. I felt such a helpless peace I would have kissed him back, had I known how. On that warm Indian-summer day in northern Ontario, I had just been given my first taste of morphine. I wouldn't turn twelve until the snow fell and melted again the following spring; by then I would have had a lot more of Paul and a lot more of his morphine. By then, I'd have learned to fix myself.

Paul was everything I was not. He was rich, had elegant features and graceful hands. He owned a new white Thunderbird convertible. Paul was also a grown man, a doctor and a pedophile. The morphine, of course, was a prelude.

Something was loosed in me that October day, something beyond blood, beyond my bantam genitals from my jeans. There is a memory so fixed and so perfect that on certain days a part of my brain listens to no other. *The top is down on his Thunderbird, the pale autumn sun warm on my skin. The blood running down my arm is like spilled roses. We are hidden from the road, partway down an old tractor trail in the grass. I am pressed against the rich red leather. Not ten feet away, yellow waxy leaves make their death rattle in the late-afternoon breeze. I am in profound awe of the ordinary—the pale sky, the blue spruce tree, the rusty barbed-wire fence, those dying yellow leaves. I am high. I am eleven years old and in communion with this world. Wholly innocent, I enter the heart of unknowing.*

For much of the winter that followed I lay face down on the couch in Paul's rec room, with my skinny white arm sticking out from under him, waiting for the next jab. I still lived at home, shared a bed with my brother, and ate my porridge with brown sugar every morning at the crowded kitchen table. I carried myself to school. After dinner, I slung my hockey bag over my shoulder and left the house waving to my mother, who thought I was spending my evenings at the rink. I can still see Paul's car, idling, with the lights out, waiting for me on the snow-packed road, the plume of the car's exhaust rising in the cold air, a curtain of white vapour I crossed through each time I went to him. That was the winter I began to disappear from my life.

Day-to-day existence became like an old photograph, faded and curling in at the edges. My body, once eager to explore every nook and cranny of the world around me, seemed now to resist the smallest of efforts. I went to Paul again and again, trying to get *me* back, trying to jam *me* back up my veins. But the more I tried, the more gaping the hole became, until so much had been spilled from me only the morphine seemed to matter. The struggle to stop my boyhood from flowing out changed to a struggle to stem the darkness flooding in—the secret self-loathing that pools in the heart of every junkie.

Paul unzipped my childhood, but it's never been as singular or as uncomplicated as blame. Mine is more than the story of a boy interrupted. It is not what Paul took from me, it is what I kept: the lie that the key to the gates of paradise was a filled syringe. In all the thousands of syringes I've emptied into my arm since then, the only gates that ever opened led to the penitentiary. Yet for most of my adult years I have clung to a deep sense of longing, a desire to return to that moment when the plunger hit bottom and the morphine arrived home for the very first time. I have staggered through a turbulent life, but I've lived that life in the arena of possibilities like everyone else. I have made countless choices along the way, broken my bones on good fortune, vandalized the best of my intentions. I have misappropriated trust, defrauded love, and found—then lost—redemption so many times you'd think I had holes in my pockets, all the while trying desperately to transport myself back to that first taste of radiance, to obliterate the dark winter that followed.

I have quit heroin to become a better thief. I have quit

heroin to become a better father, a better husband, a better friend, a better citizen. I have maintained these clean and good intentions for years at a stretch, but I have never stayed quit. It's true of men: we keep our dark secrets, hold to an unflagging belief in our manly self-will. We don't ask for directions to the corner store, and we don't ask for help in our lives. I have always returned to the needle and the spoon with a childish thirst, a self-centred insistence that I can attain utopia. The voice of the addict whispers, "Come this way, it will be different this time. Just this once, what you seek will be here." *Ad*, from the Latin "toward" or "yes," and *dict*, from the Latin "say." Addicts just say yes.

There is a Zen-like irony in the junkie slang "to fix." A shot of heroin doesn't fix anything: heroin only gives shelter to that which is broken. Blaise Pascal, the French philosopher, wrote, "Every action involves risk, possibly loss, all action leads to pain." In plainer terms: Nobody moves, and nobody gets hurt. Heroin addicts want to stop the world from spinning, to fix a point in time where it is safe—an embryonic state, the place before loss.

—

THERE WERE NINE children in our family. One died young. We moved a lot when I was growing up. The houses we rented, like the town, seemed always too small; my mother had too little money to raise too many kids. My father was away much of the time: first the Army, then the northern lumber camps, then the mines. When he came home he drank hard with his "chums," and they made the kitchen seem even smaller. I loved my dad fiercely, from the misspelled name he had tattooed on his arm the day I was born to the callouses on his hands. And I believe he loved me back in the only way he knew how. My dad would have killed Paul, but the fury he would have saved for me is what kept me silent.

At thirteen I began riding a yellow bus to the regional high school nineteen miles down Highway 17. At first the school, my circle of friends, had the gloss and mystery of newness. I attached myself to this fresh town with zeal, spending as little time as possible at home.

My secret life with Paul got easier. His house—with its plush carpets, art on the walls, a refrigerator rich with food and not one but two big, shiny bathrooms—was mere blocks from my new school. I hitchhiked home only to sleep. My dad remained absent, in one way or another, and my mom was buried under piles of laundry. I slipped away to become the ghost of my own boyhood.

Being from my hometown was like being from a bad neighbourhood. I parlayed that image into as much leather-jacket mystique as I could among the sons and daughters of merchants and mill managers. These were boys who worried about their golf scores and wore machine-knitted sweaters over houndstooth slacks. The girls had ponytails and wore Ban-Lon sweaters tucked into plaid skirts. They put pennies in their loafers and Kleenex in their brassieres.

We guzzled mickeys of lemon gin, those boys and me, in the washroom at school dances. I drank to wash down the black beauties and christmas trees I stole from Paul's bag of tricks. The gin helped kill the taste of him; the uppers quelled the nausea. When the dances ended, I would be fighting outside the New Moon Restaurant or walking one of those plaid-skirted girls home. On the sofas in their parents' living rooms, I kissed those girls too hard, then stole their mothers' tranquilizers from the medicine cabinet on my way out the door.

Paul took a vacation to Mexico and returned with poolside pictures and a bag of marijuana. He was growing leery of giving me more morphine and, I think, tiring of me. But nothing could shake my determination to extract more from him. An unspoken blackmail hung in the air between us.

Each time Paul gave me the hard stuff he'd write something in a ledger that he left on the bar. One night, high and curious, I peeked. The ledger turned out to be a mandatory account of narcotic dispensations he was obliged to keep for the RCMP. Paul had been falsely recording every cc of morphine he'd shot into me as injections to his patients.

The next day in class I kept staring at my friend Bobby M., wondering if he knew his mother was dying, afraid he'd find out I'd taken the medicine meant for her. I began to fear that everyone would learn about me and Paul. It was like living with an execution date. I started to fragment. One spring morning I missed the yellow bus. I crossed the asphalt highway and stuck out my thumb to cars heading west.

—

I LANDED ON the West Coast three years too early for the Summer of Love. In the dark heart of downtown Vancouver I had instead my first summer of heroin. In those few short months I would learn ninety-nine names for junk and lose the one for love.

Main and Hastings, the Corner: I wasn't there a hot five minutes before a young native guy turned me around so his pal could steal my gym bag. The slim contents must have evoked some feeling of kinship, because I hardly had time to notice the bag missing before they were handing it back. The first guy put his fist under my nose and told me they called him "Box," because that's what he liked to do.

Box took me for coffee at the Plaza Cafe, where there were tiny holes in the bottom of all the spoons. Box filled me in: the Chinese proprietor drilled his spoons to discourage the dope-fiend clientele from stealing them or using them to cook up in his washroom. The cops kicked the toilet doors off their hinges on a regular basis.

I'd barely had time to stir my coffee when a character everyone seemed to be waiting for strolled in the door. He wore a green suit, and his hair looked like it had been licked by a cat. Teddy Beaver was a bundle player who oversaw a small network of singles dealers. A bundle, I would learn in the weeks to come, was a package of twenty-five #5 capsules of heroin, triple-tied in a prophylactic, called a stall. I also would learn to carry the stall in my mouth, ready to swallow it at the first sign of a roust. In those days, simple possession meant a certain trip to the penitentiary.

There was a code on the Corner back then: strangers and children couldn't buy heroin. Ray Charles could see I was no cop, but Teddy wasn't going to be responsible for me being "turned out." Even after I had rolled up my sleeve and showed how Paul had already taken care of that, Teddy said he didn't want me catching a habit on his dope. It didn't matter. Box scored off Teddy, and I was "in the car."

Box scurried back to his flop with me so tight on his tail we made one shadow on the scarred red bricks along the alley. We took the back stairs of the Balmoral Hotel two at a time and hit the one john shared by all the tenants of the second floor. There was a round hole where the lock should have been; I braced my foot against the bottom of the door the way Box showed me to and kneeled to keep six out the peephole.

Box worked quickly, removing a bent spoon, an eye-dropper and the steel point of a needle he had hidden in the toilet-paper tube. He cooked the dope until the water fried at the edges of the spoon, then sat on the toilet and twisted his shirtsleeve into a knot over his bicep. When the veins jumped up, he held the dropper like a dart and sunk the needle into his arm.

Blood flagged into the dropper, and Box squeezed the bulb. His eyes closed and his body slumped against the toilet tank, the needle still hanging from his arm. I shouted his name. When he wouldn't respond, I started to shake him.

Box gradually came around enough to repeat the whole cooking ritual, and this time he sank the needle into my wing.

We spent the remains of the day in his room, sprawled across the sagging bed listening to a scratchy Chet Baker record. My tolerance was low, and I about went to heaven on less than a quarter cap. Box didn't get seasick, but me, I ran to the bathroom and spewed my junkie bile every half-hour or so.

I entered the world of Hastings Street with all the zest of a kid joining the carny. Box and I shoplifted meat and sold it to the five o'clock crowd at the Blackstone. We dry-tricked the fags over on Seymour, hustling them for ten bucks with a promise to appear. A ten-dollar bill was known as a sawbuck, the currency of the Corner. It was what the hookers charged; the price of a blow job was tied to the cost of a single cap of heroin. Box and I did whatever it took to go back to the Balmoral and get high.

Teddy Beaver appeared on the Corner every afternoon about three and stood there surveying his kingdom. One day he overheard Box ragging on me about rent. He led me by the elbow to a back booth at the Plaza for a mano a mano. I went to work for Teddy. Whenever one of his singles dealers needed to be re-upped, I would make the pickup, then the delivery. I was handling twelve to sixteen bundles a day, three hundred to four hundred caps, and yet I still couldn't score on my own.

Teddy put me away with a hooker called Kitty, whose old man had, until his court appearance that morning, worked for him. He was now sitting out a deuce-less in Oakalla. I retrieved my gym bag from Box's room and waited at the Plaza for Kitty-Cat to finish her shift. She scored two caps and we hailed a cab, stopping on Davie Street at the all-night pharmacy. KC kissed me to pass me the stall, then clip-clopped inside to grab a new kit—one eyedropper and a #26 point.

Kitty had a one-bedroom in a six-storey building on Bute. She started apologizing for the place while we were still in the elevator. Kitty was a serial apologist; she was still saying her sorrys through the bedroom door while I rummaged in her kitchen drawers for a spoon. I had cooked up and fixed half a cap before she came out in a housecoat. Kitty stood short in flat-bottomed slippers and was every inch a tender mess. I hesitated when she asked me to cook her up one cap—a cap fix was a major habit, one that would kill most users—but then I threw it in the spoon.

Before I got even half the whack into her, Kitty was into an overdose. She turned blue. I wrestled her limp body into a cold shower, where she came around slowly. It turned out Kitty's ex had been "giving her the Fraser River." It was an old junkie double-cross, which in New York would be called giving somebody the Hudson; in Toronto, Lake Erie. Kitty thought she had a major habit, but she had been shooting mostly water while her boyfriend "h.o.'d" the dope for himself.

Kitty and I fell into a routine. We kept vampire hours. Every day we woke to the setting sun, did a jimmy-hix; then she put on her high heels and painted her mouth target-red.

I put on my sneakers and we caught a cab to the Corner. She went to work at the Blackstone, me to the Plaza Cafe.

Kitty became the mirror I was afraid to look into. The heroin had us both by the throat, and I watched her skin turn grey, her bones start to jut, and sores develop at the corner of her mouth. We began to resemble the other zombie dope fiends, spiritless, single-minded in our obsession. The search for pleasure devolved into the avoidance of withdrawal. If I went without heroin for more than a few hours my nose would drip and my legs begin to ache. My quest for utopia had become a ritual of drudgery, the daily grind to maintain a habit.

One night on our way home, after she had scored our dope, Kitty announced she was pregnant. I didn't know how. She turned French tricks exclusively, and I was using four caps a day; for all the erections I ever got, she could have had swallows nesting in her vagina and I wouldn't have known. In the elevator my legs wobbled and I got a bitter taste in my mouth. The alarm bells went off, and I spit out an eight-cap stall as I slid to the floor. True to junkie form, Kitty went for the stall before she tried to help me to my feet. The stall she had forgotten to triple-tie.

I woke in St. Paul's Hospital looking up at the gentle face of a nurse. She was touching the tracks on my arms and crying. I closed my eyes, then snuck out as soon as she left the room. I waited in a blue gown at a bus stop across the street for Kitty to come pick me up in a cab. I sat on that bench, fourteen years old and so hollowed out I didn't even understand why that nurse had been so sad.

Teddy was a no-show one night, and a minor panic set in until Jerry the German went out to Chilliwack and came back with an o-zee already capped up. The word on the street next day was Teddy had been shot eight times and stuffed down a sewer grate. Rumours flew. Some said it was the Roadrunner, a notoriously vicious cop; others said Teddy had double-doored the Chinese Triads. Whatever the truth, his mother, an old east-end matriarch, spent two days and two nights out in the pouring rain, searching, until she came to the one manhole cover she hadn't wanted to find. They say the old lady lifted Teddy's body out by herself.

—

KITTY SCORED ME the first bundle I could call my own. I began putting out singles from a booth in the White Lunch. One night I was tucking a twenty in my sock, having just sold two caps to Donny-the-Poet, when two harness bulls walked in and pinned him to the floor. Behind them came the Roadrunner. He usually carried a wedge-handled flashlight to pry open the mouth of a reluctant hype, but this time he wasn't in the mood for formalities. When Donny wouldn't spit out the stall, the other two cops held him down while the Roadrunner coolly bent a fork around his own hand and began to dig his way into the Poet's mouth. Before Donny could surrender, his lips were hanging in so many shreds his mouth looked like the entrance to a car wash. On his way out, the Roadrunner warned me to sit tight, he'd be back.

I phoned Kitty from San Francisco a few weeks later. She'd had a miscarriage and was home from the hospital. The Roadrunner had come looking for me and had hung her by the ankles from the balcony. She said when he let go of her all she could think of was how glad she was she hadn't gotten the fifth-floor apartment she'd always wanted. The next time I called, her number was out of service.

I was arrested that fall outside Berkeley with a tobacco pouch full of third-grade marijuana. A judge declared me a juvenile non grata; I was flown to Seattle to await expulsion from the country. On the trip from the airport to King County Jail, in the back of the prison van, a black man tried to force me to masturbate him. We were both cuffed, and my struggles to keep him at bay amused the sheriffs no end.

The next morning an FBI agent drove me to the border crossing and turned me over to Canada Customs and Immigration. They left me unattended in a waiting room, and I bolted. I caught a ride to Vancouver and phoned my Uncle Victor, who wired me enough money to buy a ticket on the first Greyhound bus back to northern Ontario.

My mother hugged me for ten minutes straight, but it was a week before my dad acknowledged my presence in the house. I returned to school, ready to repeat the year I had missed, but my determination began to dissolve in the sea of faces in that Grade 9 classroom. My small-town values, my human values, had been forever altered. I knew things no fourteen-year-old should have to know. The days of catching snowflakes on my tongue were over.

Within months I was gone again. I got as far as Winnipeg, where I was arrested for shoplifting a leather jacket from the Bay and put in the Public Safety Building. I had a cellblock to myself. For a week I saw only a hand that set a cup of coffee and a muffin on my bars in the morning and coffee and a sandwich at lunch and dinner. Then I was sent home. My mother hugged me, my father ignored me. The ink hadn't dried on my probation papers before I was back out on the highway, my thumb hooked in the general direction of Toronto. Over the next few years, I returned to live with my parents for shorter and shorter periods. Sometimes I was brought home in the back of an OPP cruiser, sometimes I came on my own because I felt too beat-up out there.

On one trip home I learned Paul had been caught with his hands down a pair of houndstooth pants. Paul had made a mistake messing with one of their own, and the town fathers had sent him packing. During another short stay I went back to the place where Paul had parked his Thunderbird and given me my first taste, near the old Woolgemuth farm. I even fixed heroin there, in the futile hope that whatever portal had been opened on that long-ago afternoon would be opened for me again.

At sixteen I found myself back in Vancouver, back on the Corner. Two years had gone by, but I entered into the rhythm of the street so quickly you'd think I'd only been to the bathroom. I heard that Kitty had dropped some Purple Rain and gone to Haight-Ashbury to find herself. I spent Christmas that year in the solitary cells under the old cow barns in Oakalla prison for selling some bunk pot to an undercover agent.

Once I got out I went back east again, to London, where I took up with a hooker named Big Julie and acquired a methamphetamine habit. When shooting crystal got too weird, I found myself another nurse who cried over the tracks on my arms. When she ran out of tears and went back to her life, I took my madness to Toronto. Wired to the yin-yang on a $500-a-day habit, I picked up a Saturday night special.

Before Christmas of 1970, I was charged with three bank robberies. The holdup squad had beaten me so badly I had to be arraigned in early-morning magistrates' court wearing a garbage bag over my head. Don Jail officials turned me away at the front gate—I was sent to St. Michael's Hospital instead, where my jaw was wired, my broken teeth pulled, my forehead sutured, and my ribs strapped back into place. After two weeks of being handcuffed to a hospital bed, I was returned to the Don and admitted. The doctor waiting to do my intake medical, in a joyless cinderblock room, was Paul. I had heard he'd recently received five years for sexual assault and administering a narcotic to a minor, and I gathered he was being made to serve his sentence as a somewhat glorified orderly. He sat behind a bare table, wearing an ugly white smock, and went down the perfunctory checklist, never raising his eyes from my file photograph, asking questions in a monotone. When we were done he didn't ask me if I was in any pain, and I didn't ask him for any morphine. A month shy of my twenty-first birthday, a judge handed me ten years in Canada's oldest prison, Kingston Penitentiary.

My second night in the pen an old dope fiend named Suitcase Simpson hooked me up with a handful of pills. The head keeper saw me crossing the dome on the wobble and sway and ran me straight to the hole. He charged me for "condition other than normal," or CON for short. It was a charge I would see frequently, and a condition I would aspire to, for the next few years.

Prisons are about addictions. Most prisoners are casualties of their habits. They have all created victims—some in cruel and callous ways—but almost to a man they have first practised that cruelty on themselves. Prison provides the loneliness that fuels addiction. It is the slaughterhouse for addicts, and all are eventually delivered to its gates.

When we were lucky and got a package in, we used homemade rigs—syringes made from ballpoint pens and coat hangers. Other times we cooked down Darvons and cough syrup from the infirmary, or stole yeast and tomato juice from the kitchen to make a brew. We did what we could to get past the four corners of our cells.

Eventually I was transferred to a medium-security facility. I decided to throw the dope to the ground and look for another kind of escape. Within eight months I had a hook 'n' ladder play together and was living the life of a fugitive in Ottawa, where I met Paddy Mitchell and Lionel Wright; the three of us became known as the Stopwatch Gang. For the next dozen or so years, heroin ceased to be at the centre of my universe. I sipped whisky to soothe the beast, but I was too busy to chase a dope habit. We stole millions of dollars, racked up nine escapes among the three of us, and made the most wanted list in two countries. By Hallowe'en of 1980 the FBI had caught up with me in Arizona. They dragged me off to the ultimate penitentiary: Marion, Illinois.

Four years later I was transferred to Canada. I had grown bone-weary of prison culture and my criminal lifestyle. I went to my cell one day, closed my door, and began to write. When my head came up a year later, I had the first draft of a novel. I sent the manuscript to Fred Desroches, a criminologist at the University of Waterloo, who passed it on to their writer-in-residence, Susan Musgrave. Susan became my editor, then my wife, in a maximum-security wedding. I published *Jackrabbit Parole*, and a year later I was released.

We moved to Vancouver Island, to a vine-covered cottage by the sea. I bought a weed eater, and a pink bicycle for my stepdaughter, Charlotte. I planted annuals. I began to engage with a new matrix of friends; I planted perennials. For the first two years I fixed up our home, pounding nails and painting trim. Susan and I had a second daughter, Sophie. I began another novel but found myself staring for hours at a blank page. I had been released from prison, but still I had not escaped. I felt the same profound aloneness in the midst of my warrant-burning party in our garden as I had in my Grade 9 class. Once again I went in search of the only solace I knew.

—

THE ONLY REAL serenity I have ever experienced, paradoxically and tellingly, has been without the assistance of drugs. It arose from a long period of abstinence, late in life, encouraged by the love of my wife and my daughters, nurtured by my friends, and witnessed by a God of my understanding—in whom, ultimately, I could not extinguish my addiction.

Even after a lifetime, I was not done with my crimes, nor were they done with me. In 1999 I returned to a full-blown heroin and cocaine habit. I had tried to keep a foot in each world, to hold on to the weight of love and family, but I was pulled into the underworld of drugs. I chose to destroy both lives—not in a calculated way, more by default, but a choice nonetheless. I committed the worst bank robbery of my life, an unprofessional, unnecessary act of violence. It cost me an eighteen-year sentence, and nearly cost some people their lives.

Now, at fifty pieces, I find myself stripped bare, beaten back from hope, all out of illusions, in yet another prison cell. Having fallen through the crust of this earth so many times, it seems that only on this small and familiar pad of concrete, where I can make seven steps in one direction, then take seven back, do my feet touch down with any certainty.

A year before my arrest, when Sophie was nine, we went out sliding after a freak snowfall. Hurtling down the hill on a red plastic saucer, we whirled faster and faster until the edge caught and we spilled. We tumbled through the snow, Sophie's pearly whites shining to the heavens, her laughter like small golden bells.

Now Sophie is twelve. When she accompanies her mother on their weekly visits to the prison, I hold her on my lap, and those wide brown eyes fix onto mine. Sophie needs to see me rise up again, return to her life. Though we are connected in unbreakable ways, I worry about her memories of a drug-addicted dad.

So I pace, seven steps one way, seven steps back. And I write. The days pass. I sit on my concrete pad, cross my legs, and begin to breathe. The darkness of my world melts away, and as I move toward the mystery of mysteries, I can almost hear those faint golden bells. Slowly I enter the heart of unknowing, without expectation, without heroin.

AFTERWORD

A MONTH AFTER I wrote my essay for this book I lay in my front hall, flopping on the hardwood floor like a salmon on the bottom of a boat. Two days later I went into a residential treatment program. For the next eight weeks, I spent sixteen hours a day stumbling through group therapy, AA meetings, confused sessions with my counsellor, and endless conversations with other drunks and addicts.

Every morning in that place I got up into the last of night so I could drink thin coffee and have a cigarette outside in the smoke pit, alone except for the watchful night staff and a few ghostly inmates who walked the halls mumbling to themselves. One early morning I saw a full moon as I walked the narrow path from my room to the main building to begin another hopeless day. I was detoxed, but I didn't know who I was. I knew I wasn't in prison, yet it felt like it. I knew I could walk away any time I wanted, yet I was afraid, terrified of leaving. I remember stopping in the middle of the path and looking up at that pale fire in the sky. It was just the moon, you understand. Yet I remember standing there, still, and then I lifted my arms and said to the night and the stars and that glistening, distant moon: I give up. I surrender.

And I did.

After almost fifty years of addiction I was finished.

The essays in this collection are not confessions. It would be too easy to call them that. Maybe each is a kind of witnessing to a life lived at both ends of a burning candle. If the words help someone survive, then this book will do what Lorna Crozier and I want it to.

In December of 2000, the first of the millennium, the *Globe and Mail* asked me to write a piece about Christmas. I was barely a week out of treatment and still pretty shaky. I include it here to remind myself of who I've been and who I am now. I think of the people I went through treatment with. Seven months after this piece's publication, six of them were dead, and the plaque on the wall of the treatment centre read a little longer.

THE WORLD CALLS us drunks and addicts. The people here call us chemically dependent. What we call ourselves is mostly unprintable. The counsellors tell us we have a disease. The woman next to me, a sweet nineteen-year-old, is an anorexic heroin addict who's been hooking on the street since she was eleven. Beside her is a young man who started dealing crack cocaine in Grade 8 to pay for his habit. He was on the street at fifteen, selling his body every few hours for a hundred or fifty or sometimes twenty quick bucks and beaten a hundred times in rooms and alleys. The drunks are older. It can sometimes take a while to hit bottom from liquor. But most of the drunks are addicted to other things as well: crystal meth, Ecstasy, Tylenol 3, Valium, amphetamines, hash, crack cocaine, heroin.

We're all standing around a forty-foot Christmas tree singing carols, something we didn't do when we were lying in our lonely rooms with a bottle, a pipe or a needle. We're here for seven or eight weeks or longer. Some of us will stay for a year or more. Right now none of us are thinking of the plaque on the wall outside listing the dead addicts and drunks who came through here. We're singing Christmas carols as loud as we can and drinking pop, coffee or tea as we stare at the tree, that old pagan image of the solstice. Some of us will be dead in six weeks or six months and some of us will live a while longer. It's Christmas in treatment and the only family we have is us, our shared disease, this addiction that has driven us past despair to this place of compassion and confrontation.

We sing "Jingle Bells" and follow it with "The First Noël." Most of us are tough people who can laugh or cry at will. Con artists, naive dreamers, romantics and fools, most of us have lived on the street at one time or another, but here, in this season of apprehended joy, there is just a hope there might be something more than what we've got. Around us are the whispers of the past, families and loved ones, some of whom still care and some who can't any more. But the season here isn't sad. We're too frightened to be sad, too frightened to be lonely.

We sing as hard as we can. The tree glistens with lights. There is a strange, surreal happiness in the room. It is a time for song and no one thinks of the night to come, the stunned tears in the dark, the fear that moves hidden among us. A boy-man beside me sings along to "Rudolph, the Red-Nosed Reindeer" and we all join in with laughter at how silly we are. Yesterday was the first time this man wore a short-sleeved shirt. White scars crawl like worms on his arms. He is getting past his shame.

A young woman hiding behind a post sings softly, shyly, with her eyes half closed. She is someone's daughter, someone's lover. I would take her hand if I could. I would tell her everything will be all right. But I can't do that. The odds are things won't be okay ever again. She's only a step away from a room of crack pipes and seizures, a broken bottle in the back seat of a car, a needle hanging from her arm. She's only a step away from being clean, too, but that's a big step, and I don't know if she'll take it.

It's Christmas. There's a tree and many lights and people singing. Some of us will make it, some of us won't, but we sing our hearts out anyway. We sing as hard as we can.

PATRICK LANE

ABOUT THE CONTRIBUTORS

TOM BISSELL is a journalist, critic, and fiction writer. He was born in Escanaba, Michigan, in 1974, and graduated from Michigan State University before briefly serving in the Peace Corps in Uzbekistan. Bissell is a recipient of the Rome Prize and also a Guggenheim Fellowship. His short stories and journalism have also been anthologized in *The Best American Short Stories*, *The Best American Travel Writing* and *The Best American Science Writing*. The many magazines he has written for include *Harper's*, the *New Yorker*, *Grantland*, the *New Republic* and GQ, among many others. He lives in Los Angeles.

SUSAN CHEEVER is the author of fifteen books, four of which are memoirs. These include *Drinking in America* and the bestselling *Home Before Dark*, a memoir about her father, John Cheever. Her most recent work is *My Name is Bill*, a biography of Bill Wilson, founder of Alcoholics Anonymous. Cheever has written for many publications, including the *New Yorker* and the *New York Times*; she currently teaches writing seminars at Bennington and The New School in New York City.

LORNA CROZIER has published a memoir, three books for children and eighteen collections of poetry; the latest are the 2015 publications *The Wrong Cat* and *The Wild in You*, a collaboration with photographer Ian McAllister. An Officer of the Order of Canada and a Fellow of the Royal Society, she is the recipient of several national awards, including the Governor General's, and five honorary doctorates for her contributions to Canadian literature. She has read her poetry on every continent except Antarctica. She lives on Vancouver Island with poet Patrick Lane and two fine cats.

For the original edition of this work, PETER GZOWSKI wrote: "Peter Gzowski has been the editor of more magazines than many people have read, the host of more radio and TV programs than many people have listened to or watched, and the embarrassed recipient of more lifetime achievement awards than most people have lifetimes. Father of five, grandfather of two, he is the winner of an East Coast Music Award (mostly for not singing during the breaks) and once came second in one of his own golf tournaments for literacy, which are now held in all ten provinces and all three territories of Canada. He has never been to Zagreb but has been to Aklavik seven times. He is an ex-smoker." Peter died in 2002 of chronic obstructive pulmonary disease.

MOLLY JONG-FAST is the author of *Normal Girl* (2000), *Girl [Maladjusted]* (2004) and *The Social Climber's Handbook* (2011).

She has written for many newspapers and magazines, including the *New York Times*, *Harper's Bazaar*, *W*, *Travel and Leisure*, *Cosmopolitan*, *The Times (UK)*, and *Marie Claire*. She is married to a recovering academic and has three not-that-small children, all of whom like to talk to her when she is on the phone. She lives in Manhattan.

The guest of poetry festivals all over the world, PATRICK LANE has been called the best Canadian poet of his generation. In praising his selected poems, the *Vancouver Sun* described him as always walking "the thin ice where truth and terror meet with a kind of savage intuition." He is the author of twenty books of poetry, most recently *Go Leaving Strange*, one collection of short stories, and one children's book; he is the co-editor, with Lorna Crozier, of *Breathing Fire 1* and *Breathing Fire 2*. His memoir, in Canada titled *There is a Season: A Memoir in a Garden* and in the United States *What the Stones Remember*, received the 2005 British Columbia Award for Canadian Nonfiction and was nominated for the annual Barnes & Noble Discover Great New Writers Award for nonfiction. A novel, *Red Dog*, was published in 2008. A new collection of poems, *Washita*, was nominated for the Governor General's Award in 2015.

EVELYN LAU was born in Vancouver in 1971. She is the author of a memoir of her adolescence, *Runaway: Diary of a Street Kid*, which was published when she was eighteen. It became a bestseller and was made into a CBC-TV movie starring Sandra Oh. Evelyn has since published two short-story collections, a book of essays, a novel and four volumes of poetry. Her prose works have been translated into a dozen languages around the world.

LESSLIE was born in 1973 in Duncan, British Columbia, as a member of the Coast Salish nation. His colonized, Catholic, Canadian name is Leslie Robert Sam. lessLIE is his decolonized artist's name. Picasso once said "art is a lie that tells the truth." lessLIE is living this perspective in the spirit of trickster traditions. He has a Bachelor of Arts degree in First Nations studies from Malaspina University-College, and he is working on a Master of Arts degree in interdisciplinary studies with a focus on Coast Salish art at the University of Victoria.

ELIANNA LEV is a writer who lives between her hometown of Toronto and her spiritual happy place, Vancouver. Her essays have been published in the *National Post*, *Lucky Peach*, *Flare*, *Elle Canada* and *Vice*. Her blog is called *I'm a Good Story*, and she is currently working on her first book, *Sex Made Me*.

JOHN NEWLOVE (1938-2003) was born and raised in Saskatchewan. His many honours included the 1972 Governor General's Award for his book *Lies*, and the Saskatchewan Writers' Guild Founders' Award. His works have been internationally published and translated. His posthumous *A Long*

Continual Argument: The Selected Poems of John Newlove (2007), edited by Robert McTavish with an afterword by Jeff Derksen, is the comprehensive statement of an acknowledged poetic master craftsman.

STEPHEN REID's *Jackrabbit Parole* (reprinted in 1999 and again in 2015) is an autobiographical novel of a gang of bank robbers (The Stopwatch Gang) who escaped once too often. In 2013 a collection of his essays, *A Crowbar in The Buddhist Garden*, won the City of Victoria/Butler Book of the Year Award. Recently released from prison, he currently lives on Haida Gwaii with his wife, the poet Susan Musgrave. He continues to write.

DAVID ADAMS RICHARDS was born in Newcastle, New Brunswick, and lives in Toronto with his family. He is one of the few writers in the history of the Governor General's Award to win in both the fiction, for *Nights Below Station Street*, and the nonfiction, for *Lines on the Water*, categories. In addition to these two wins, he was nominated for *Road to the Stilt House* in 1985, *For Those Who Hunt the Wounded Down* in 1993 and *Mercy Among the Children* in 2000. Considered by many to be Richards' most accomplished novel, *Mercy* was co-winner of the Giller Award in 2000, and was shortlisted for the Trillium Award and the Thomas Raddall Atlantic Fiction Award.

LOIS SIMMIE is an incorrigible genre-hopper, having written long and short adult fiction and radio drama; children's picture books, poetry collections, and plays; and a historical true crime book, *The Secret Lives of Sgt. John Wilson*, which won the Crime Writers of Canada Arthur Ellis nonfiction prize. Her adult fiction includes the novels *They Shouldn't Make You Promise That* and *What I'm Trying to Say is Goodbye*, a work about quitting alcohol, among other things. Her children's titles include *Mister Got to Go Where are You?* and *Mister Got to Go and Arnie*. She lives in Saskatoon where she is working on her memoir.

RICK WHITAKER is the author of *Assuming the Position*, *The First Time I Met Frank O'Hara* and *An Honest Ghost*, a 2013 novel that consists entirely of sentences stolen from other books.

SHERI-D WILSON (aka The Mama of Dada) is an internationally recognized spoken word poet. She has performed and led workshops in Canada, the United States, England, France, Mexico and South Africa. She is the author of nine collections of poetry; her most recent, *Open Letter: Woman Against Violence Against Women* (2014), was nominated for the 2015 Robert Kroetsch Poetry Book Award and her collection, *Re:Zoom* (2005), won the 2006 Stephan G. Stephansson Award for Poetry. Her work has received national and international acclaim. She won the USA Heavyweight title for poetry in 2003, and in 2006 The National Slam of Canada presented her with the Poet of Honour Award. Sheri-D received the 2015 City of Calgary Award for her contribution to the Arts.

MARNIE WOODROW is the author of two novels, *Heyday* and *Spelling Mississippi*, and two short fiction collections. She lives in Hamilton, Ontario.